CHILD ABUSE REVISITED

CHILD ABUSE REVISITED
Children, society and social work

DAVID M. COOPER

OPEN UNIVERSITY PRESS
Buckingham · Philadelphia

Open University Press
Celtic Court
22 Ballmoor
Buckingham
MK18 1XW

and

1900 Frost Road, Suite 101
Bristol, PA 19007, USA

First Published 1993

A catalogue record of this book is available from the British Library.

Library of Congress Cataloging-in-Publication Data

Cooper, David Michael.
  Child abuse revisited : children, society, and social work / David M. Cooper.
    p.   cm.
  Includes bibliographical references and index.
  ISBN 0−335-15727-0   ISBN 0-335-15726-2 (pbk.)
    1. Social work with children−Great Britain.   2. Child abuse−
Great Britain.   I. Title.
HV751.A6C664   1993
362.7'6'0941−dc20   92-19315
                                                                CIP

Typeset by Colset Private Limited, Singapore
Printed in Great Britain by Biddles Ltd, Guildford and Kings Lynn

CONTENTS

PREFACE

On my office wall is a cartoon showing a man standing separate from a group of others at a party. Their comment about him is: 'He hasn't written a book about child abuse.' Perhaps there may be something to be said for not being one of the crowd in this matter. Yet child abuse is too important not to be writing about.

This book will, I hope, find a place somewhere in the lists because it has a very distinctive perspective. It does not claim to be one of those essential reviews of evidence and research works that we need from time to time although it is as generously referenced as I can manage; nor is it a book that deals much with specific treatment of abused children or individuals who maltreat them, for others are much better qualified than I to write about such things.

What it does offer are perspectives for looking at the way we have defined child abuse and at the patterns in our response to it. Abuse comes in many forms and we need to understand how we select our priorities for action. If not, and this is the passionately held theme of the book, there is a real danger of a loss of objectivity and that is not good for children. In this matter the work is as important as the source of abuse. Hence social work figures prominently throughout because it says so much about the attitude of the state and society to children and even childhood itself. If there are any 'answers' to child abuse then they are to be found in the wide view, through binoculars rather than through microscopes.

ACKNOWLEDGEMENTS

Writing a book is an organic, incremental process and it is never clear where and when it starts. Apart from the quoted references there are many sources that may be lost to consciousness but which are just as vital. For that reason I pay tribute to the many academic colleagues, social workers and students who, by working with me, have wittingly and unwittingly stimulated my thinking about this tragic but fascinating thing we call child abuse. More particularly I thank Norman Jenkins for his comments on Chapter 1, Sue Amphlett for permission to use so much Parents Against INjustice (PAIN) material, the Open University for permission to use the case study 'Edward's Story' from *The Children Act 1989: Putting it into Practice* (1991), David Whitehouse for typing so well and with such helpful interest, and finally Hilary and Kristy for lots of tea and even more tolerance.

approximately 9 per cent of the English child population. In 1988 they were replaced by national figures collated from returns from local authority social services departments:

(at 31 March)	1981	1985	1989 (All England)
Emotional abuse	4	22	2000
Sexual abuse	27	222	5900
All abuse	1176	1586	40700

The term 'higher order' may be objected to in relation to emotional and sexual abuse because they will be seen as very damaging to children. This is not disputed, but it is not the point here. By their nature these forms of abuse are difficult to detect and treat; they take time and expertise, things which may not be available in poorer societies grappling with subsistence problems. It is evident that these higher order sufferings are also legitimated concerns. The Children Act 1989 defines significant harm very widely to include 'physical, intellectual, emotional, social or behavioural development' and ill-treatment which encompasses 'sexual abuse and forms of ill-treatment which are not physical' (Section 31(9)).

Whether these developments in affluent societies are appropriate is a matter for debate. There is strong evidence that our policy assumptions about basic abuse are misguided. An underclass of poor families appears to be growing steadily (Cohen, 1988; Oppenheim, 1990) for whom higher-order child care is far from easy. Bradshaw in his report on UK child poverty, commissioned by UNICEF, refers to concerns that in the last ten to fifteen years the 'well-being' of children in some industrialized countries, as well as in the Third World, may be declining (1990, p. 1). It is ironical too that our affluence allows us to worry about forms of abuse that poorer societies cannot even begin to consider.

Comparative abuse

Even amongst the richer nations in Europe there are considerable differences in attitudes towards child abuse despite the growing influence of European Community legislation (see Sale and Davies, 1990). Germany may have under-recorded abuse in the past partly because 'registration has a quality of denunciation reminiscent of the Nazi period', and in the Netherlands 'statutory agencies and the police are only called in as a last resort' (Sluckin and Dolan, 1989, p. 15). By contrast the UK and USA have welcomed more vigorous state intervention and close collaboration between police and social workers. Again the UK, unlike the USA and Canada, has no national reporting laws which require anyone to notify the authorities of abuse if they encounter it.

National attitudes towards sexual activity and children also vary. Laws regarding sexual consent reveal that for heterosexual, homosexual or lesbian contact Belgium, Germany, Ireland, Luxembourg and the UK are generally more restrictive societies than their European neighbours (*The Independent on Sunday*, 29/9/91, p. 4). Similarly, physical punishment of children reflects different attitudes. Unlike the UK, Austria, Denmark, Finland, Norway, and Sweden forbid parents from chastising their children and the UK remained until 1986 the only European country to allow beatings as part of school discipline (Roche, 1989, pp. 138–9.)

We see then a picture of abuse developing along with affluence. Expectations grow and uncover new concerns which require new definitions. Whatever these concerns are they generate great anxiety, particularly because they disturb affluent societies' sense of well-being and comfort; they form an intolerable paradox. This anxiety has to be dealt with at psychological, social and political levels.

Attributing child abuse

A large amount of political and social science theorizing is about laying blame – on capitalism, on Marxism, on attitudes, ideologies, systems and structures. The way blame has been laid for child abuse is an essential part of understanding how the UK has explained and responded to the phenomenon in the last twenty years.

Williams (1989) has summarized the ways in which writers have classified different perspectives on welfare problems:

- Anti-collectivism – a focus on individual responsibility and choice, the importance of the private and voluntary sectors and a reduction in direct state services.
- Social Reformism – various levels and styles of socialist intervention which seek to improve and re-design the welfare state within present society.
- Political Economy of Welfare – the Marxist analysis that sees unmet need as inevitable within a capitalist system.
- Feminist Critique – an approach which requires the resolution of gender inequality as a pre-requisite for other structural changes.
- Anti-racist Critique – an approach which gives priority to the power relationships between different ethnic and cultural groups in society.

Each of these perspectives can have an impact on child abuse both conceptually and empirically and will reappear in this book. Historically, the social reformist position has been strong in the UK since 1945, this being based on a broad political consensus and an active welfare state that provided both services to families and protection of children against their parents. By the 1970s the earlier political consensus was disintegrating and, as well, social scientists, alarmed by the resurgence of poverty, were seeking more radical solutions than social reformism could offer. Marxist analyses, whilst attractive, offered few short-term suggestions and have thus had very limited influence on welfare policy.

As Williams argues (Chapters 3 and 4) feminism and anti-racism have brought important new challenges to social science perspectives and their influence on child abuse is still to be evaluated (see Chapter 4.) This leaves anti-collectivism as a way of viewing social problems and a central argument throughout this book is that this perspective has had a major influence on child abuse in the last thirteen years. Since 1979 the New Right have emphasized the responsibility and central role of the individuals in child care. This has been accompanied by a reduction in direct state services in favour of a privatized system of voluntary and other care. Along with the radical values of the anti-collectivist perspective come important changes in welfare structure. The coming implementation of care in the community will separate the *purchase* of services from their *provision*; this could lead to the break-up of a state child-care system which has existed since 1948.

As well as the concept of child care service, the focus of policy has changed significantly. Hardiker et al. (1991) have talked of state welfare intervention within what they term *residual, institutional* and *developmental* models to correspond with low through to high involvement. The residual model would offer 'a basic minimum as a last resort/safety net' (p. 19) and would also conceive of social workers as agents of social control where the work is 'judicial; rescue the victim, punish the villain' (p. 32), at a tertiary level where abuse has already taken place.

Protection and regulation

Hardiker's developmental model would envisage wide-ranging pro-active state policies designed to promote family living as a way of helping children. However, as the next chapter will analyse, legislation in the last twenty years has not gone in this direction and thus the operant definition of child abuse has been far less broad than this book proposes. Instead the residual model has sought justification in an individual pathology (Sheppard, 1982) view of child abuse which then requires social control from social workers. This contrasts with social workers' own aspirations. The Barclay Report (1982) envisaged a wide role from individual counselling through to social care planning and with a special emphasis on developing community social work. In child-care terms these aspirations have been disappointed. Where there has been a growth in social work activity it has been within the largely anti-collectivist framework.

Parton (1985 and 1991) has analysed these developments and especially the idea of 'dangerousness' which is seen to reside in individuals – mainly parents but also, on occasion, social workers and other workers involved in child abuse. Regarding this method of attribution he says:

> Similarly, the centrality of a binary classification based on dangerousness has become even more explicit in the political economy of the 1980s, for while the state is rolled back in some areas it is strengthened in others. The role of the state is not so much reduced as re-directed. It is the notion of dangerousness which provides the criteria whereby such a sifting is to be articulated and legitimated. (Parton, 1991, p. 203)

Thus there are families who cope (i.e. who do not come to official notice) for whom state services have declined and then there are families who are 'dangerous'. They attract social work attention of a particular level.

The moulding of state social work into the form of social control required by the residualist model has been one of the most striking features of the last ten years. A series of highly publicized child killings committed by their carers put considerable pressure on the Government to 'do something'. The death of Maria Colwell in 1973, and of Jasmine Beckford and Kimberley Carlyle in the mid-1980s (DHSS, 1982; DoH, 1991a) have produced increasingly detailed official regulation of child care workers and agencies (see especially *Protecting Children*, DoH, 1988 and *Working Together*, DoH, 1991b). The Children Act 1989, which will be discussed in the next chapter, is accompanied by *nine* substantial volumes of *Regulations and Guidance*, and sets out procedures for emergency protection of children in far more detail than any of its predecessors. Although this regulation of activity extends also to the provision of services to families it is generally set out more loosely.

More recent child abuse inquiries have introduced new themes. Whereas social workers were initially criticized for *under-reaction* to events, the concern now is with *over-reaction*. In Cleveland, both paediatricians and social workers allowed medical assessments and a pre-occupation with 'rescue' to bring around 120 children into care via emergency court measures. Later events in Rochdale, Nottingham and Orkney reinforced a public and government view of further social work mistakes.

In order to cope with what is, in effect, criticism of state services the Government has had to distance itself from social workers just as employers might deny responsibility for deviant employees. Ideologically, this has not proved difficult. Certainly the Government has appeared willing to allow more than forty official inquiries to take place at considerable cost – Beckford around £300,000, Cleveland £2 million, and the most recent in the Orkney Islands (concerned with only *nine* children) is costing around £100,000 weekly with a final bill estimated at around £7.5 million (*The Independent on Sunday*, 24/11/91, p. 3). These costs, though substantial, are small compared with funding large-scale improvements in preventive family services. A feature of *all* the inquiries is that their brief has been limited to *events and actions leading to individual tragedies*. Where wider issues have surfaced, such as under-funded services or poverty and discrimination, they have not been widely publicized either by the media or the Government. The blame therefore has remained attached to individuals; children have been seen as at risk rather than more generally in need because of structural failures.

Because child abuse inquiries have received so much publicity they have become symbols. They make a statement about something going wrong in society and we have argued that the governmental view of what this is has greatly influenced the way the inquiries were used. However, this is an incomplete explanation. The process whereby society was *ready* to respond as it did suggests something more complex than just politics.

Moral panic and modern anxiety

Why exactly did the Maria Colwell inquiry in 1974 provoke the public out-cry it did? Just a year before, an investigation into the death of another child, Graham Bagnall, passed by with almost negligible publicity. What were the psycho-social elements that produced such a strong reaction, one that had the social worker involved verbally and physically abused on her way into the inquiry and later led her to change not only her job but also her name?

Hall et al. (1978) offered a sociological analysis of this kind of public reac-tion, a moral panic as it was termed, in their study of concerns in the UK about mugging. Parton (1985) has adapted some of the conclusions to child abuse. Hall says:

> It is as if each surge of social anxiety finds a temporary respite in the projection of fears onto and into certain compelling anxiety-laden themes: in the discovery of folk-devils, the mounting of moral cam-paigns, the expiation of prosecution and control – in the moral panic cycle. (p. 322)

and again:

> Politically in Britain, as elsewhere, the 1968–69 period represents a watershed: the whole fulcrum of society turns and the country enters, not a temporary and passing rupture but a prolonged and continuous state of siege. (p. 251)

The elements of a moral panic are thus a breakdown in general consensus, intense social anxieties, the need to lay blame and the search for culprits or scapegoats. As Hall also argues, in such circumstances governments are active in trying to direct public anxieties and anger along certain paths and we have already commented on this in relation to parents and social workers. We shall examine the recent development of social work in Chapter 3 and argue that it is not merely an unfortunate victim of outside hostility, but has contributed to its own difficulties.

Government manipulations will only flourish in fertile ground. We argue that the high degree of public anxiety evident when Hall's study was undertaken still exists and may even be stronger, leading to an authoritarian element which is also discussed by Hall in a later work (1980). These anxieties may arise from several areas: Britain's changed world role, economic decline, the gap between individual dreams and realities, and massive changes in personal roles and family structure.

A feature of post-war Britain has been a tension between the nostalgia for an imperial past and the sharply different realities of modern politics. This nostalgia was evident in the Falklands War of 1982 and the rhetoric and public excitement that surrounded it. The images of 'Britain standing alone' and 'Britain ruling the waves' resurfaced vividly only to sink again. A related ambivalence about Europe, never far below the surface of government statements also reflected the tension between past and present.

The second element of economic decline is also well documented. The general post-war improvement in living standards has been achieved at the cost of widening gaps between rich and poor and the growth of a new underclass that does not easily fit within earlier class frameworks. As unemployment has become an intrinsic feature of the economy this group has expanded and become alienated from mainstream society. Gortz has termed them the 'non-class of non-workers' (Keane and Owens, 1986, ch. 9), and because they are so difficult to understand from earlier positions, they are a barely expressed threat to society.

We are a society of dreams purveyed by powerful media, and especially television. Allied with an economy dependent on consumerism, the public has become conditioned to expecting a lifestyle which will continually improve. The accelerating rate of knowledge in science and technology and the development of information technology generate an impatience with the present and a demand for the future at once. Television, with its powerful, fast-moving images shows that the world really is our oyster but also the dire penalties if we do not succeed. The influences cannot be overstated, particularly in relation to public opinion. As Postman (1985, p. 80) argues: 'Television has achieved the status of "meta-medium" – an instrument that directs not only our knowledge of the world, but of *ways of knowing* as well.' The miracles have become more and more vivid but so have the villains. While economic growth continued it could be said that the gap between the promise and the reality was tolerable, but as the 1980s continued, this was clearly no longer the case.

Personal and family role changes have mirrored the demand for change. Hoggett and Pearl (1991, chs 6 and 12) document the rise in divorce and the subsequent effects on children and their parents. The number of divorced couples in England and Wales doubled between 1970 and 1989 with the rate per thousand rising from 6 in 1971 to 12.7 in 1989. There has been an increase in joint custody following divorce, but also an increase in sole custody awarded to mothers who far outnumber fathers in this respect. Access issues may act to sustain relationships which were dead and buried although evidence shows that the great majority of couples do make amicable arrangements to the great benefit of their children. However the number of step-families has inevitably grown with men having to set up new 'father' relationships with someone else's children. This is significant in the light of Finkelhor et al.'s finding (1986, pp. 77–9) that the presence of a step-father is significantly correlated with sexual abuse.

Some idea of the psychological complexity is conveyed by Brenda Madox, quoted by Hoggett and Pearl (1991, p. 556):

> Who we are depends entirely on two families – our family of origin and our family of procreation; we are the children of our parents and the parents of our children. But we are not told how to preserve our sense of identity if we have a mother in one family, a father in another, a son in a third and a daughter in a fourth.

Changes in family structure also require changes in personal roles. Added to these are changes in employment and unemployment. Feminism has also had a major impact on gender perceptions. Much of it may be latent in terms of actual redistribution of power in society but its psychological effect on women and men should not be underestimated. Domestic violence is a serious problem; in as many as 44 per cent of killings of women the suspect is or was married to the victim (Home Office Circular, 1990). We may be at a transitional stage where awareness of their rights may be making women less willing to remain in bad relationships with men, but unable, because of lack of education, social support or money, to actually break free. Men, in their turn, may perceive a threatened loss of old ways of behaving without understanding an acceptable alternative.

Do these sources of stress and anxiety breed violence? Certainly we are more violent than in the immediate post-war past. In 1990, there were 676 killings in England and Wales compared with 347 in 1946. All crimes rose from 500,000 in 1950 to 4.5 million in 1990. Men mainly commit these offences and all the 241 women killed in 1991 in Britain were victims of men. On the other hand, 99 victims were under 16 years and in 29 of these cases mothers have been charged or convicted. Of the UK 1991 total of 708,300 killings involved a domestic dispute. Perhaps a small consolation is that we are around seven times less violent per capita than the USA where the 1991 total of killings was over 24,000 (*The Independent on Sunday*, 12/1/92 pp. 1 and 15).

Racial inequality continues to contribute to family and personal stress. Ethnic minorities generally are over-represented in poverty, youth (and thus juvenile crime) unemployment and illness as well as suffering direct racial harassment. Although this will vary from culture to culture black young people may also suffer difficult identity problems and the situation of mixed race children appears to be particularly acute (Bebbington and Miles, 1989). For all this, black people are slowly becoming more visible in daily life – in television, in newspapers, magazines and in jobs; they are also beginning to move out of the big cities. (Cheetham, 1986, p. 12 quotes census figures to show that in 1981 around one third of the Asian population and over half of West Indians lived in the Greater London area.) A concern, though, is that if the present economic recession continues, racism may become more overt and violent as white people feel more threatened and seek scapegoats (see Aronson, 1984, for American experiences).

see p. 4.

The above discussion indicates that our society has not generally become more tranquil as people have become better off. If anything the opposite has occurred, perhaps because the growth of consumerism and especially the explosion of credit debt in the mid-1980s fostered an 'easy come easy go' attitude. Also, better living standards for many people were only possible if they worked harder, which created greater child-care problems and less leisure time in families. Thus a frequent companion of success was anxiety with regular media reports of spectacular financial frauds and company collapses.

Consumerism is essentially a lonely individual philosophy with little time for communal values. Fear of failure in a world which almost seemed to expect success may have led to tendencies to attribute blame more readily. Litigation, public inquiries and media witch-hunts have become common features of modern life, echoing Hall's description of moral panic. When failures involved children's lives the flood of social anxiety and insecurity followed this same pattern and the search for scapegoats began in earnest.

Blaming social workers

Aronson (1984, p. 251) says 'The general picture of scapegoating that emerges is that individuals tend to displace aggression into groups that are disliked, that are visible and that are relatively powerless.' In the early 1970s social workers were becoming more visible as the new social services departments enjoyed relatively good growth and an expansion of their influence. As a consequence they were also beginning to question structural issues and thus made enemies. The Children and Young Persons Act of 1969 greatly increased the power of social workers, and in the case of juvenile crime, at the expense of magistrates. In this climate it was the expansion of services rather than the refinement of child protection which had priority.

The eruption of the Maria Colwell Inquiry Report in 1974 into this atmosphere brought massive criticism of social workers. They were alleged to be too sympathetic to the parents of Maria Colwell to give the child first priority (Packman, 1981). Around the same time an influential study by

Rowe and Lambert (1973) suggested that children in care were in need of more rigorous and vigorous plans for their future. Media treatment exaggerated this careful research to suggest that social workers were preventing thousands of children being placed in good permanent homes by refusing to sever unproductive birth family ties (Holman, 1988, pp. 67–72).

Despite their growing influence within local authorities, social services departments had little power in either professional or wider political terms. Thus the third characteristic of the scapegoat applies and there is little doubt that the process has continued. Although successive child abuse inquiries have included other workers – health visitors, teachers, doctors and police – in their criticisms, it is social workers whose treatment, especially in the media, has been the harshest with a second much bigger wave of hostility following the Beckford Report (London Borough of Brent, 1985).

The intensity of hostility towards social workers suggests complex psychosocial factors at work and this is to be expected in the dynamics of a moral panic. The Government's action, conscious or not, of distancing itself from its social work agents enabled the public to displace its anger and fears from the whole state to just a part of it, a simpler and safer option. In 1987, the Central Council for Education and Training in Social Work (CCETSW) sought approval and fairly modest resources to increase basic training from two to three years; the Government brusquely rejected this request. Instead of *enhancing* social work it apparently preferred to *regulate* it by the introduction of increasingly detailed procedures and guidelines through the 1980s.

Perhaps a final part of the moral panic jigsaw is the inherently uncertain nature of social work itself. Even within the workforce, definitions have regularly fluctuated between social reformist and individual counsellor. Jordan (1987) talks perceptively of social work as an official body which operated in 'everyday relationships' where there is 'intimacy and pain' and without 'the characteristics of the higher status professions' (pp. 207–8). This unique role which is social work's greatest value and strength may also be the one which doomed it to become society's scapegoat.

Aronson's (1984, especially chs 2, 3 and 4) wide-ranging review of social psychology makes a number of points which are relevant here about communication relationships and the status of the sender. If we consider how social workers communicated their child care work to the public before the death of Maria Colwell we have a situation where a relatively low-status group was routinely pointing out that children suffer for complex social reasons and that there were no simple solutions. Because of social workers' low credibility in the communication sense, the public could reduce its 'cognitive dissonance' (Aronson, 1984, pp. 116–23) by mostly ignoring such messages. However the impact of the Colwell case was such that this was no longer a sufficient device, for the appointment of a format inquiry panel chaired by a non-social worker (and thus with more credibility) made the message impossible to ignore. The dissonance reduction strategies employed by the public to ease their own alarm about child-rearing were more easily accomplished because of the unique character of social work and the scapegoating referred to earlier in this section was thus possible.

The perception of social workers in child care as an ambiguous and ambivalent group is echoed again by Louis Blom-Cooper, a lawyer who chaired both the Beckford and Carlyle Inquiries:

> Social workers present to the journalist a prime target for the good story. They operate in a field of competing social motives; they are insufficiently rigorous in their practices; they appear to be sympathetic to wrongdoers; they are politically biased, perceived as predominantly left-wing to a press that is heavily tilted in the other direction; and they are gullible to every sob story. (Blom-Cooper, 1991, p. 136)

Golding in the same publication (1991) reviews the long-standing discussions about social work's public image and concludes that the picture is a confused one and that: 'In short, there is strong evidence to suggest that the public likes what social work does, just not who does it and who gets it!' (p. 96). This analysis of the confused public image of social workers makes it easier to understand why criticism of them could so easily shift through the 1980s from under-reaction to over-reaction.

The present state of child abuse

I began this chapter by arguing for a very broad definition of child abuse. However it appears that social, political and operational attitudes have led to a much more partial and selective view of the problem. Events through the 1980s have conspired to locate abuse in the realm of parent failures, compounded by inadequacies in the state child protection service. The thrust of government policy has been to strengthen the residual protective elements of state social work while reducing its family and developmental services. Parents themselves have responded to this change by making less voluntary use of social workers (see Cooper and Ball, 1987, ch. 1) and regarding them as threatening intruders.

The argument for the present system is that greater state alertness has uncovered previously hidden levels of abuse by carers and has prevented injury or death. Although this cannot be quantified with certainty it has some validity, particularly in the area of sexual abuse. The Maria Colwell tragedy did indicate that sound child care practice had perhaps been diluted by the wider challenges of post-Seebohm social work with its interest in social and structural factors. National Society for the Prevention of Cruelty to Children (NSPCC) figures show that the numbers of seriously or fatally injured children recorded on the registers declined between 1977 and 1984 from 17 to 8 per cent (Creighton, 1984) and this may indicate the benefits of greater vigilance. Yet the increase in protective vigilance led, almost inevitably, to the excesses of Cleveland.

Social work, like its host society has moved steadily from consensus to conflict in its child care practice. In terms of our wide definition of abuse this policy and practice needs to be balanced by services which promote the welfare of children within their families. At present these come mainly from voluntary agencies which, with the exception of the NSPCC, have maintained their central focus on prevention. The balance between prevention and protection is crucial to help children and one way to ensure this is through legislation. The next chapter will therefore review the relationship between child care legislation and child abuse.

2/

LAW

Frameworks for analysis

This chapter echoes the previous one in adopting a broad definition. With regard to the law, it is *child care* rather than child abuse which is the appropriate term; in fact child abuse has not been used in legal terminology at all although it does appear once as a section heading in the latest legislation (Children Act, 1989, Schedule 2, Para. 4.) The concerns of child care law have generally been threats to children's welfare and how to reduce them as well as what services are needed to promote welfare; thus the twin themes of promotion and protection occur and recur.

More specifically the factors in question have been and still are parents' actions, state actions and children's rights and these can be viewed positively or negatively. So legislation could focus on reducing state powers if they were a threat to children or increasing them to promote welfare, and the same would apply to parents' activities. Children's rights are not straightforward; it might be that increasing them could raise difficult protection issues. These themes will be explored within two frameworks; first, a set of perspectives developed by Harding (1991) and secondly, a complementary set proposed by the author to identify five main areas of concern in legislation.

The first part of the chapter will consider the period 1933 to 1989 and the main child care legislation enacted then. The second part will analyse in detail the important new Children Act of 1989 which was implemented in full in October 1991. These areas are well covered in the literature: Packman (1981) reviews much of the earlier period; Holman (1988) provides additional analysis with an emphasis on preventive themes; Hoggett (1987) has a concise and comprehensive summary of the law that existed until just before the new Act; Parton (1985) considers law in terms of child abuse developments and updates it (1991) with a sophisticated analysis of political and other factors which contributed to the present position; Hoggett and Pearl (1991) provide a wealth of case law, comment and information about all aspects of law relating to children and families; the 1989 Act is described in manageable form by Allen (1990) and with more legal analysis by Bainham (1990).

Perspectives on law

Harding's important contribution has been to apply a set of perspectives to child care policy and legislation both in conceptual and empirical terms. Hence:

(a) *Laissez-Faire and Patriarchy* – common until after 1945, characterized by limited state intervention in family life; based on a belief that parents (especially fathers) have the right and duty to manage their children free from interference except in extreme cases.
(b) *State Paternalism and Child Protection* – showing a willingness to increase state intervention for all children and especially those at risk within their families. This leads to a reduction in parental privacy and autonomy.
(c) *Defence of the Birth Family and Parents' Rights* – A partial reaction to (b). Different from (a) because it also advocates active state intervention to promote family life.
(d) *Children's Rights and Child Liberation* – a more recent perspective which advocates action to increase children's rights as individuals and to reduce their vulnerability to either parents or the state.

This framework is valuable in encompassing history, attitudes and policy, although its use of 'paternalism' in (b) relates less to men than does 'patriarchy' in (a). These are perspectives, not positions, and Harding does not see them as mutually exclusive. Despite its value this framework cannot always be applied in a simple and comprehensive way to child care legislation so we propose an extra framework which considers legislation under five areas of concern:

1 The promotion of facilities for families.
2 The protection of children from families.
3 The provision of substitute care (mainly by the state).
4 The promotion of children's rights in the broad sense.
5 A concern with juvenile crime and offenders.

This framework produces the chart below (Fig. 2.1). The 1933 Children and Young Persons Act is omitted because it reflects pre-war state welfare agency organization but Harding has described it as:

a huge consolidatory act which developed further the provisions for both young offenders and children in need of care and protection. As well as consolidation, the Act includes some innovations, such as the extension of the powers of local education authorities and probation officers, and more emphasis on welfare. (1991, p. 89)

The chart reveals the way the law has addressed different issues at different times and this needs to be considered in relation to contemporary social, political and economic circumstances. The 1948 Act had a very specific aim, to set up a specialist service for children deprived of a normal family life in the wake of war-time turbulence. By 1963, and with growing prosperity, the Children's Departments had grown secure and confident enough to be expanding their work into prevention of child abuse, and the Act of that year formally endorsed this area to the extent of allowing cash to be offered in exceptional circumstances to keep children out of state care and/or away from courts. 1969 brought a unique Act which not only extended the 1963 legislation regarding child protection but also redefined juvenile crime by those under 14 years as simply *one* aspect of child deprivation and which required treatment rather than punishment. This fusing of welfare and justice approaches was radical and was accompanied by a proposal to raise the minimum age of criminal responsibility from 10 to 14 years.

The 1969 attempt to see juvenile crime as a welfare issue was defeated with the election of a new Conservative government and the age of criminal responsibility remained, and still remains, at 10 years. This illustrates that all legislation, to some extent, has enemies. In the previous chapter we argued that social work's growth around this time was not universally welcomed and the 'law and order lobby' was successful in diluting the full impact of the 1969 Act. As Fig. 2.1 shows, since that bold experiment juvenile offenders have again been separated from other children and affairs dealt with under criminal justice provisions.

By 1975, in the immediate wake of the Maria Colwell inquiry, concern had moved from promoting the welfare of the birth family to increasing state intervention and strengthening regulations regarding children in substitute care. Inroads were made into parental rights by increasing the grounds for taking protective action, by allowing courts to decide that children could be separately represented from their parents in court cases (although this was not fully implemented for nine years!) and by making it more difficult for parents to recover their children from *voluntary* care after six months.

This period also witnessed the emergence of children's rights. Apart from the right to separate representation in court which included the opportunity for children to instruct their own solicitors in certain cases, the 1975 Act introduced the requirement that children's wishes and feelings should be considered when they were in substitute care and being considered for adoption.

Figure 2.1 Child care legislation 1948–89: main areas of concern

	1 Promoting work with families	2 Protecting children from families	3 Substitute care by the State	4 Children's rights	5 Juvenile offending	
Children Act 1948	* →		* →			Children and Young Persons Act 1933
Children and Young Persons Act 1963		*			* ↓ → *	Criminal Justice Acts 1982, 1988 and 1991
Children and Young Persons Act 1969		← ─┘ *	* →			
Children Act 1975		*	* →	* →		
Adoption Act 1976				* →		
Child Care Act 1980	* →	* →	* →	* →		
Children Act 1989	→*	→*	→*	→*		

Notes: * Concern applies to Act

↗ Concern incorporated into other Acts

In the matter of voluntary family services it was still assumed that their wishes coincided with those of their parents.

The chart also reveals the importance of the 1989 Act. Excluding the 1980 legislation, which was essentially a device to tidy up and consolidate previous Acts, we can appreciate the huge scope of the new Act, covering as it does all the key areas of child care except juvenile offending. Not only does it update and revoke all earlier legislation, but it also redefines child care provisions following the breakdown of parental relationships and sets out a comprehensive court system for all cases involving children.

The 1989 Act takes a much wider look at children's situations. Disabled children are given the umbrella protection of legislation which they had previously lacked and a coherent system is introduced for local authority oversight of children living away from their families in all other forms of substitute care from hospitals to independent schools. While the 1975 Act took first steps in considering children's rights it is the new Act which deals with them as a central principle and this will be analysed in a later section of this chapter. A final fundamental innovation of the 1989 Act is its acknowledgement that in a multi-cultural society children's background must be actively considered. Thus, at various points there is reference to cultural, linguistic and racial factors, as well as the religious ones of earlier legislation.

Harding's perspectives can also be seen from our chart. While the 1963 Act was clearly designed to support birth families, the 1975 Act marked an increase in state intervention through child protection. The 1989 Act is more difficult to interpret because it *appears* to reflect all four perspectives, though minimally so in the case of *Laissez-Faire*. It is also worth noting that *there was no new preventive legislation between 1963 and 1989*. As we showed in the first chapter, the period in question saw various public inquiries but these were mainly concerned with protecting children from their parents. In 1974 the Finer Report on One-parent Families expressed serious concern about levels of poverty and stress and the need for structural and economic changes. The fact that these findings did *not* lead to relevant legislation supports our earlier arguments about the prevailing political climate of the last twenty years.

Both of the frameworks used here are useful but they lack an important element. They fail to include the idea that *performance* of state intervention is an issue as well as the *level of intervention*. This brings us back to the view that the Government, from a distance, has been concerned about the activities of its agents, the local authority social services departments. Such a perspective can put a different light on child care legislation. It could be argued that developments since 1975 are concerned not so much with children, parents and the state as such, but with regulating the activities of social workers per se. In this light, therefore, measures which appear to increase the rights of parents, for example, may be negatively rather than positively conceived. Perhaps it doesn't matter if it brings benefits anyway but it does add a different dimension to the analysis.

Whatever the approach, what is evident is that the 1989 legislation is a fundamental and fascinating climax to post-war child care policy. Whether it marks an end or a beginning of a new era will now be explored.

The Children Act 1989

'In need' or 'at risk'

Chapter one argued that children can be abused in many ways, but recent history has preferred to focus on parents and carers as the main culprits. Where does the new Act fit into this pattern? Although it certainly addresses the need to provide services to families as well as protection from families it has not provided *a common definition* for both kinds of situation. This has received little comment yet it may be crucial in evaluating the motives and impact of the legislation.

In Section 17(10) of the 1989 Act the following appears:

For the purposes of this Part a child shall be taken to be in need if:

(a) he is unlikely to achieve or maintain, or to have the opportunity of achieving or maintaining, a reasonable standard of health and development without the provision for him of services by a local authority under this Part;

(b) his health or development is likely to be significantly impaired or further impaired without the provision for him of such services; or

(c) he is disabled,

and 'family', in relation to such a child, includes any person who has parental responsibility for the child and any other person with whom he has been living.

and Section 17(11):

a child is disabled if he is blind, deaf or dumb or suffers from mental disorder of any kind or is substantially and permanently handicapped by illness, injury or congenital deformity or such other disability as may be prescribed.

(In passing it is sad to see the discredited and insensitive word 'dumb' associated with deafness. Otherwise vigorous campaigners for anti-discrimination have drawn little attention to this blatant example.)

The part of the Act which includes this central definition of 'in need' is concerned exclusively with *voluntary services* for children and families and thus the term can *only* be applied legally to the failure or absence of such services under this part of the Act. This is an acknowledgement, then, that children can suffer at the hands of the state and the definition of 'in need' is commendably wide in its emphasis on their development. Thus:

> 'development' means physical, intellectual, emotional, social or behavioural development; and 'health' means physical or mental health. (Section 17(11))

If adequate services are not forthcoming a form of redress is offered in Section 26(3), although this is phrased in such a way that the emphasis is on the procedure rather than on the actual right to complain. Children, parents and certain others can make representations or complaints to the local authority although it is not clear what further legal rights exist if the outcome does not satisfy the applicants. Nevertheless the Act is much more specific than its predecessors in defining what services should be offered.

'At risk' of 'significant harm' is defined elsewhere in the Children Act, in Section 31(9) and (10). This is within Part 4 of the Act which is concerned with longer term court orders although the definition also applies to Part 5 of the Act entitled 'Protection of Children'. The definition includes present and likely future harm although only the latter can be applied in emergency situations. Where care and supervision orders are being sought (by local authorities or the NSPCC under the present law) the court should only grant such orders if satisfied:

(a) that the child concerned is suffering or is likely to suffer significant harm; and
(b) that the harm, or the likelihood of harm is attributable to –
  (i) the care given to the child or likely to be given to him if the order were not made, not being what it would be reasonable to expect a parent to give to him;

or

  (ii) the child being beyond parental control. (Section 31(2))

The awkwardness of the phrasing indicates the problems being faced by lawmakers in holding parents to account without writing them off as bad or useless; it is more a question of a standard of care that is or is not reached. However, Freeman (1991) comments that ' "attributable to" is different to and much broader than "caused by" ' and 'The reasonableness criterion makes no allowance for parents who are incapable of meeting the reasonableness hurdle' (p. 19).

The definition of 'significant harm' is cast in the same wide terms as 'in need' and this would seem to be an important protection for children. However, if we compare the overall tone of Parts 3, 4 and 5 of the Act it is evident that the phrasing and definitions of the first are less prescriptive and detailed about what to do when things go wrong. At the same time, and this has received less publicity in the literature than one might expect, the definition of significant harm *as it applies to emergency situations* would allow *anyone* to seek a court order to remove a child from danger or prevent him/her being moved into danger. This is very important because it could apply as much to a child in local authority foster or residential care as one living at home.

Against this, what could be done if the state is deficient in providing services seems to merit less attention. Nine volumes of detailed guidance and regulations have been issued along with the Children Act and these do have the effect of making local authorities more accountable. But only so far: the duties to provide services set out in Schedule 2 of the Act abound with let-out clauses such as 'shall take reasonable steps', 'as they consider appropriate' or 'as are reasonably practicable'. Section 23(8), in defining services for disabled children requires that accommodation provided by the local authority shall be 'so far as is reasonably practicable' . . . 'not unsuitable to his particular needs'. Can we detect a political distinction between 'suitable' and 'not unsuitable'?

It appears then that what may be 'reasonably' expected from the state could be less than what may be expected from parents. The latter would have considerable difficulty defending themselves by arguing that it was not reasonably practicable for them to provide proper care of their children because, say, they were living in poverty. Furthermore, the legal recourses available to parents and to the state differ. Except in the case of emergencies the state can use well-defined court measures whereas parents have to make do with local authority complaints procedures. Even before this new Act, courts were reluctant to support parental action against local authorities (see the judgement in *A. v. Liverpool City Council*, 1982) and now the use of wardship proceedings in the High Court has been further restricted.

Earlier we commented that the 1969 Act was unique in trying to bring together juvenile justice and child protection. The 1989 Act had a similar opportunity to acknowledge the width of child abuse by creating one all-embracing definition that combined 'in need' with 'significant harm'. It would have been a very complex task to do this effectively but it would have been a fundamental demonstration that the child's interests really are 'paramount', as the Act asserts. As it is, the message seems to be that the state, in legal terms, is a priori reasonable whereas parents may not be. How well is this borne out by evidence of the increased poverty and hardship of poor families and the risks to children of being looked after by under-funded authorities?

Children's rights

Whereas there may be some fundamental ideological doubts about the commitment of the 1989 Act to children's welfare, it has pioneered, at a lower level, the principle that children's *rights* should be a central theme. If we accept that child abuse reflects a power imbalance then this principle may contribute to their protection.

Eekelaar, quoted by Hoggett and Pearl (1991, pp. 432–33), suggests that children have three kinds of interests: *basic interests* concerned with safety and general well-being, *developmental interests* centred around the ability to achieve potential, and *autonomy interests* in having some control over their lives. All three are threatened by child abuse and all three are acknowledged by the 1989 Act. Basic interests have always been protected and developmental interests are now better codified in this Act than before because of its emphasis on future significant harm and its wide definition of development. The new emphasis on cultural, linguistic and racial factors will also further this interest.

It is in the area of *autonomy interests* that the new Children Act is most significant. Although the 1975 Act introduced the importance of seeking the opinions of children, this applied mainly to children in care. Indirectly, children could also express their opinions because of the new provision in that Act to allow children to be separately represented against their parents in court cases. The Cleveland Report (Secretary of State for Social Services, 1988) has been influential in extending this issue because of its central finding that the state was as capable as parents of ignoring children's views.

Thus the 1989 Act seeks to develop children's rights in two ways: first, by viewing that in certain circumstances, their wishes and feelings should be discovered, where practicable; secondly, defining specific situations where the child can take legal action to seek or resist major changes in his/her circumstances. In most cases the child must be of 'sufficient understanding' to exercise these rights except in two situations where a minimum age is stated (see Fig. 2.2).

To enable children to exercise their rights in court the Children Act has greatly extended the use of Guardians-*ad-litem*. However their prime duty is to discover and recommend what the child *needs* rather than what he/she *wants*. If the two do not coincide the child's power to appoint his/her own solicitor independently protects these rights.

References to the child's cultural, linguistic and racial background are also well represented in relation to court hearings (except emergencies), 'looked after' children, local authority and private day care, childminding, local authority foster parents' attitudes, voluntary organization accommodation and private children's homes. Excluded from the references are residential care, nursing homes and independent schools.

It appears then that the Children Act is both firm and thorough in its concern for children's developmental interests and autonomy. Whether this automatically increases protection against abuse is a more difficult question. The broader debate about children's rights is beyond the scope of this book but is well reviewed in Franklin (1986), Bainham (1988, ch. 3), Roche (1989, ch. 14), Harding (1991, ch. 5) and Hoggett and Pearl (1991, especially pp. 428–37). What is clear as events in Cleveland, Rochdale and the Orkneys illustrate is that the desire to protect children has not always met with their approval. The new rights to refuse assessment and examination complicate the task of social workers. We live in a litigious society and older children are becoming more articulate consumers. The seeds planted in the Children Act will produce welcome blooms but they are likely to need careful tending and may create new complications.

Evidence rights

A frequent concern in child abuse prosecutions has been that prosecution of alleged abusers has often failed because of the legal weakness of children's evidence. This has applied especially in sexual abuse where physical evidence is rarely available and the child's statements are therefore crucial.

Until recently children under seven were unable even to offer evidence in criminal proceedings. More generally judges were required to explore whether the child was 'competent' to give evidence. The Criminal Justice Act 1991 (Section 52) abolishes these restrictions and for the first time allows courts to permit any child who can communicate intelligibly to give evidence. Following the recommendations of the Pigot Committee (Home

Figure 2.2   Extracts from the Children Act 1989

Discovering children's wishes and feelings	
Children Act 1989 section	Circumstances
1(3)(a)	In all court proceedings except emergency protection and child assessment cases.
20(b)	Where *plans* are being made for a child to be 'looked after' by the local authority.
22(4)(a)	Where *decisions* are being made where 'looking after' is being contemplated and is already taking place.
24(4)(c)	Where after-care is being offered.
26(3)(a)	In representations and complaints about local authority services.
46(3)(d)	When the child has been taken into 'police protection'.
61(2)(a) & (3)(a)	When the child is being accommodated by a voluntary organization.
64(2)(a) & (3)(a)	As above in relation to a private children's home.
Schedule 3 12(2) & (3)	When a supervisor is planning 'directions' under an Education Supervision order.

Figure 2.2   *continued*

Children's legal powers	
Children Act 1989 section	*Specific power*
4(3)(b)	To challenge parental responsibility rights over the child acquired by the unmarried father.
10(8)	To make an application (with the court's agreement) for a Section 8 order.
20(11)	*If over 16 years* to request local authority accommodation or to request to remain in it regardless of the parents' wishes.
26(3)(a)	To make representations or complaints about local authority services.
34(2) & (4)	To request a Contact Order or request that a Contact Order be refused while the child is subject to a Care Order.
39(1)(b) (2)(b)	To apply for the discharge of a Care Order To apply for the variation or discharge of a Supervision Order.
41(4)(b)	To instruct a solicitor in public law court hearings.
43(12)	To apply for the variation or discharge of a Child Assessment Order.
45(8)(a)	To apply for the discharge of an Emergency Protection Order.
Schedule 3 17(1)(a)	To apply for the discharge of an Education Supervision Order.
Also	*To refuse to be assessed, examined or receive treatment under:*
38(6)	An Interim Supervision or Court Order.
43(8)	A Child Assessment Order
44(7)	An Emergency Protection Order
Schedule 3 4(4) & (5)	A Supervision Order
N.B.	In addition the importance of listening to children is regularly stressed in the guidelines that accompany the 1989 Act

Office, 1989) video-recorded evidence will be used but the Act nevertheless required that in such cases that the child can be cross-examined though from the relative protection of a separate room via a 'live link' (National Children's Bureau/Barnardos 1991). In civil cases it has long been possible for children's statements to be relayed by adults and the Children Act confirms and extends this practice.

Weighing up protection

Over- and under-reaction

The 1989 Act develops important new concepts and measures to protect children. As we have indicated this frequently relates to significant harm and thus, in practice, to parents as the threat. How successful is the Act likely to be in this respect?

After around twenty years of child abuse inquiries the themes that are visible are under-reaction, more recently over-reaction, and throughout the problems of inter-agency collaboration (see Cooper and Ball, 1987). In all these aspects the new Act makes important contributions. In terms of over-reaction courts are under a strict duty not to remove children unless orders will improve their condition; thus the mere proof that abuse has or is likely to occur is not sufficient to guarantee the making of an order. Criticisms of social workers' use of emergency powers and court provisions have produced legislation which 'is permeated with lawyers' logic' (Freeman, 1991, p. 18). As well the new Child Assessment Order offers a less drastic method of assessing a child's condition that will not normally require removal from home.

Parents and carers have new rights to challenge decisions in emergency situations and their right is secured for party status with consequent eligibility for legal aid. There is also provision for parents to contribute to their children's assessment; this is important in cases where for example medical evidence may be open to second opinions. The development of the Guardian-ad-litem service and their increasing expertise may also contribute to a more measured assessment of social worker's evidence; this will also be more open to scrutiny in 'Directions' hearings held before the main hearing, with the purpose of reviewing each party's position. The patterns established by these pre-hearings will have an important influence on court outcomes. Even after court orders have been granted the new law assumes reasonable contact between children and parents unless there are special arguments otherwise. There are also general requirements on local authorities to consult and inform parents regarding plans and decisions about their children.

In terms of under-reaction the Act is clear in expecting social workers to respond vigorously to allegations of child abuse. By including in the definition of significant harm, the notion of future danger, investigation can be more broadly based although this will inevitably provoke challenges in the courts about the art and accuracy of prediction. The new Child Assessment Order might be seen as a measure to limit the use of the more serious Emergency Protection Order but per se it is a new form of intervention that extends the range of social workers' powers to protect. As an extra precaution, courts can, in their own right, convert an application for the lesser order into one for the greater.

The Act is reinforced in considerable detail by a battery of guidelines, especially, in Volume 1 as well as the Department of Health publications *Protecting Children* (DoH 1988) and *Working Together* (1991b). Their themes are essentially that child protection work should be systematic. thorough and detailed and they seem to bear out Parton's view (1991, chs 5 and 6) of a legalistic process which, while giving social workers a central role, puts strict controls on their activities.

One value of regulation is that it can enable better understood and co-ordinated practice. This has been a regular wish of child abuse inquiries, and the Children Act accompanied by the 1991 version of *Working Together* clearly sets out the role, functions and tasks of all the main workers and agencies in child abuse. Other state agencies (although significantly excluding the Department of Social Security) are now *required* where possible to co-operate with social services departments in Sections 27(1) regarding services to families and 47(9) regarding emergency protection.

One thing that is still absent in the UK is any system of mandatory child abuse reporting law which would make it an offence for anyone not to pass on information. However, as Dingwall et al. suggest (1983, pp. 11 and 231–2) this provision may be of limited value in practice because it is almost impossible to monitor.

In private as well as in public law the 1989 Act grants important protective powers to courts. Section eight orders which can determine where the child lives and with whom he/she has contact as well as other measures, can be made unasked, at the court's discretion. When their concern is greater they can request full investigations by the local authority (Section 37). This should normally be completed within eight weeks and, significantly the local authority must give full reasons if it does not recommend a care or supervision order and even specify what alternative help it proposes to offer to the child in question.

Controls on parents

The Government asserted that the Children Act offered a great deal to parents and expressed the principle of non-intervention. This is perhaps true in terms of specific rights to challenge local authority decisions but it is more questionable overall. One of the Act's most radical innovations was to create a class of 'persons holding parental responsibility' who have equal status with 'parents' in most cases, adoption being an exception. Rights are re-defined as merely something acquired through parental responsibility in order to bring up children properly, and for no other reason. Hence parents under the Children Act are always 'on trial'. If they are good parents they can expect to be left alone, but if they are not there are numerous points at which the law will intervene.

The general principle of previous legislation that home was where the child ought to be is now subject to conditions. Even where there is a duty to provide services to families it is; *'so far as is consistent with that duty*, to promote the upbringing of such children by their families' (Section 17(1)(b); italics added). Similar references to the family occur where the child is being looked after by someone else.

I have already referred to the significant harm test and 'attributing' the child's problem to parental behaviour. Within emergency situations, protec-tion is further strengthened by the inclusion of a new provision (Section 47(6)). If parents unreasonably refuse to co-operate with social workers' investigations by refusing entry or information about their child this is a suf-ficient ground for court orders to be applied for.

If we add to these measures, the increased rights of children to be heard and to seek remedies on their own behalf then it can be argued that the posi-tion of parents is carefully regulated by the Act. The guidance documents previously described also make greater demand on *all* workers and agencies to share concerns and report suspicions and this is likely to increase surveillance of parents.

White (1990, p. 749) has also commented on some new measures which can exert control over parents and other carers. Section 8 orders in the Act will allow courts to give directions about how these orders are to be carried out in relation to where children live, what contacts they have and other mat-ters. This power would enable courts to require 'an adult to act in a certain way (as distinct from refraining from so acting,) a power which even the per-vasive wardship jurisdiction was hesitant to assume'. A similar pattern is available where supervision orders are made, although here the adults must give their prior consent to conditions.

It is obviously too early to tell how and how much the courts will use these new powers, and it remains to be seen how the new concept of parental responsibility will translate into practice. As a clear sign that children do not exist at the whim of their parents it is an important protection against abuse. Increased children's rights may also encourage young people to demand local authority accommodation on their own behalf and to protest more firmly and, hopefully, to be heard and listened to, when they feel threatened by decisions about their lives.

A criticism might be that the family in the very narrow sense of parent–child is at the centre of child care and needs careful protection and promotion. It is on this point that the 1989 Children Act may prove to be less impressive than its rhetoric. Services to families are cast as the first level of protection against abuse, yet this legislation carries with it no extra allocated money; nor can it be seen as the expression of a new social policy initiative designed to reduce pressure and deprivation in young families. Without this element the position of parents, under the Act, appears much less secure.

Controls on local authorities

Since 1988 and the Cleveland inquiry a spate of well publicized 'scandals' have further sharpened public concern that the state itself through its agents, can be abusive to children, and this has come to be known as 'system abuse'. It can occur both during investigations and while children are in local authority care.

Sexual abuse investigation has attracted particular attention because, by its nature, it may be difficult to detect. The first area of concern has been the use of so-called 'disclosure' interviews, particularly by social workers. These occur when it is suspected a child may have been abused but is reluctant for various reasons to admit it; the interview style will therefore be aimed at encouraging a 'disclosure' by the child.

The Cleveland inquiry dealt with this matter at length (ch. 12) and concluded that the very terms 'disclosure' is dangerous because it pre-judges the outcome and can exert great pressure on children. Even so the term was still used in Rochdale and the Orkneys and our impression is that it remains common among social workers. The Children Act makes no specific reference to this matter of interviewing in abuse investigations and *Working Together* is surprisingly brief about it, being content to say: 'All referrals, whatever their origin, must be taken seriously *and must be considered with an open mind that does not pre-judge the situation*' (DHSS, 1986, para., 5.11.1; italics added).

Paragraph 5.14.7 sets out the principles of good interviewing but says little about the dangers of exerting undue pressure. Yet, as Bannister and Print (1988) show, such interviews are very difficult for social workers in trying to reconcile forensic and therapeutic aims.

The overall style of child abuse investigation has also been questioned. Police and social workers usually collaborate from the outset, and if, as Parton argues, child protection has become more legalistic, then the forensic considerations have assumed greater importance. In Rochdale in 1990, twenty children from six families were taken into care jointly by police and social workers in controversial 'dawn raids' because of allegations of ritual abuse. All except four were later returned home and Rochdale social services (and the police) were heavily criticized for their handling of the matter (*Social Work Today*, 23/1/92, p. 7).

In a subsequent report into the Rochdale child protection service, the Social Services Inspectorate commented on: 'a widespread practice in the North-West and elsewhere of calling on families early in the morning which requires further investigation' (1990, para., 5.13).

The report acknowledged the real dilemmas for the protection services and recommended that when the original version of *Working Together* (DoH, 1986) was revised that it should address these issues. However, as we have seen, the 1991 version deals fairly briefly with them even while acknowledging the problems of investigating organized abuse (paras 5.26.5, 6 and 7).

Abuse in care

Being in care is rarely easy for children. They arrive with serious problems often which can hamper social work plans for them. The need to consider rehabilitation with their families, which is re-affirmed by the Children Act is a further complication despite the value of the principle. Once in care children may suffer placement disruptions (see Marsh, 1989, ch. 6) as well as sometimes poor quality care in foster homes or residential homes. Parker (1990, ch. 4) reviews local authority staffing figures from a 1986 survey; these show that whereas 85 per cent of field workers have social work qualifications, in residential child care the figure was 14.5 per cent. Whereas fieldwork levels had steadily risen through the 1970s they had remained 'substantially unchanged' (p. 37) in residential care.

Since the Children Act was drafted, two 'scandals' have brought widespread public attention to residential child care. The 'Pindown' affair in Staffordshire was officially investigated (DoH, 1991d) after concern about oppressive regimes and methods used against children. In 1991, in a separate affair Frank Beck was sentenced to a long prison term for offences committed against young people in local authority homes between 1974 and 1986. These incidents will in time produce further government regulations and guidelines.

The 1989 Act has broken new ground in developing a wide range of regulations and guidelines to apply to all situations where children are in substitute care whether foster parents, hospitals or independent schools. Local authorities will undertake these duties and although they represent greater protection for children there is, as usual, the major question of resources if monitoring and investigation are to be effective. Much substitute care is of good quality despite the sensational sins of a tiny minority of carers. However, the new Act at least provides a firm base and clear procedures for increasing protection to children who cannot live at home.

Summary

A number of frameworks and perspectives have been introduced as a means of making sense of child care legislation since 1945. We have considered first the major laws from that time until 1989 and identified the most significant trends and the historical events which influenced them. The second longer part has examined the 1989 Children Act as a measure to protect children against abuse. Children's rights, the control of parents and the control of local authorities have been assessed and we have also suggested that the State's desire to restrain social workers in particular is also a factor. While it would seem that as a coherent piece of legislation the new Act has made an important contribution against abuse it may prove to be seriously undermined. In the crucial area of services to families the duties laid on local authorities are too often conditional and, in the end, dependent on resources. The Act was implemented during a period of severe economic recession in the UK under a government which is unable or unwilling to initiate any major campaign of centralized prevention to assist young families at risk.

Whatever the outcome it will be state social workers who continue to carry the main legal responsibility for promoting and protecting the welfare of children in need. The next chapter will therefore examine the development and present position of this group of workers in the child care field.

3 / SOCIAL WORK

The importance of social work

Social work has figured frequently in the first two chapters. Here we propose to consider its background, its development and its present condition; we shall also make some cautious predictions about its future.

Is this effort justified? The answer is that social workers, particularly in the state sector are very important to children at risk and only a little less so to children in need. The forty or so official child abuse inquiries would presumably agree with the first statement although their interest has only arisen negatively when things went wrong. Nevertheless the Children Act 1989 reaffirms that local authorities through their social services departments will continue to play a central statutory role in child care.

Another reason for studying social work is that, in sociological terms it is an interesting phenomenon. Social workers form an occupational group which lies uneasily between the status quo, the establishment and the reformist left, a group which has relatively little professional influence, yet has often been criticized as if it wielded great power. These ambiguities are nowhere more clearly stated than in the *Basic Code of Ethics* (BASW, 1986). Here there is reference to professional aspirations, obligations to employers, realistic limitations and concern for global rights, work with individuals, groups and communities from counselling to social planning and action, to individual tolerance through to 'challenging' discrimination.

What the social worker's job is remains a matter of dispute. Howe (1991, p. 204) says:

I remain impressed with analyses which reveal social work to be largely a state-sponsored, agency-based, organisationally tethered activity. It is not wise to tackle any examination of social work without taking note of this formidable context.

In the same book Sibeon quoting Young says:

> according to Young there is no identifiable or definable 'professional social work' that floats free of *particular* organizational objectives and purposes in the varied service-delivery contexts in which social workers are employed. (1991, p. 61)

This would seem to argue more clearly what social workers are not (free-floating professionals) than what they are. This is understandably difficult but perhaps a sensitive and realistic definition is offered by Jordan (1987, p. 207):

> Yet social workers' potential strength lies in their ability to be effective mediators in situations where other officials would struggle. Precisely because they do not possess the characteristics of the higher-status professions (exclusive knowledge, awesome professional territory, exclusive decision-making power) they *have* to learn to work in unpromising situations – in often chaotic environments, making decisions over which they can be challenged by lay people or a number of other officials.

Yet as we shall see later, others have imagined social workers as being either hard-line revolutionaries or dedicated therapists, with various stopping points in between. Certainly the social worker's bed-fellows are varied: the police in child abuse, therapists in family work, volunteers in service arrangements and community workers in development action projects – and this has not made either their public image or their own self-identity easy to pin down. Altogether then social work is well studied as perhaps a reflection of contemporary society and social policy.

A short history of social work

Social services departments and radical social work

Any historical account of social workers tends to have a built-in assumption, namely that their position in child care has been generally different from, and more troublesome in relation to other client groups.

The 1960s witnessed a considerable growth in social work child-care activities (Packman, 1981) in an era of economic expansion and broad social and political support. This came with the 'welfare' philosophy of the Children and Young Persons Act 1969 and the creation through the Seebohm Report (1968) of the new local authority social services departments. They had a generic 'open-door' policy and social workers, especially from the best-qualified children's departments became prominent in key positions.

The 1970s brought two key developments for social work which proved

to be incompatible and resulted in a winner and a loser. The new departments were much larger than the previous constituent ones and the economy
of scale welcomed by Seebohm also created much larger bureaucracies and
the growth of managerialism (Cooper, 1982). On the other hand, this period
also saw the growing influence of sociological approaches and the idea that
the economic and social circumstances of clients needed addressing
vigorously (see Pearson, 1975; Corrigan and Leonard, 1978; Simpkin,
1979). Yet this same period also included the death of Maria Colwell in 1973
and the English public certainly were not inclined to believe that better child
protection lay down the road to Marxism.

If revolution failed to arrive it left traces in the related, more modest
movements towards 'patch systems' (Hadley and McGrath, 1980). This was
a method of making social work more localized and accountable to clients
and their communities and required decentralized organizational structures.
The Barclay Report (1982) was an attempt largely by social workers to
review their position and point the way forward. Although it contained
dissenting voices, it envisaged a wide role for social workers from counselling to social care planning and particularly identified community social
work as a major development to be pursued.

A number of social services departments sought to implement some form
of patch system, East Sussex for example, and there was a widespread
interest in what seemed a flexible and open approach to service delivery
based on a recognition that clients needed more say in their affairs. The
movement also made important statements about the role of voluntary agencies and informal networks which anticipate some of the current principles
of care in the community.

Retrenchment and the growth of child protection

History indicates that patch approach never really took hold of social services departments particularly in its more radical form. Three linked reasons
are suggested. First, economic growth had come to a halt in the mid-1970s
and the days of ambitious developmental work were numbered. Secondly,
more child abuse inquiries continued their depressing litany of criticisms of
social work. Thirdly, the Conservative Government of Mrs Thatcher came
to power in 1979 and introduced a right-wing residual philosophy of state
welfare; this inevitably preferred a role for social workers, especially in child
care, through 'social policing'. Ironically this Government also embraced the
idea of an enhanced voluntary and informal care section, but for somewhat
different reasons than patch system advocates.

The rest of the 1980s has already been explored in Chapters 1 and 2. Concerns about child abuse continued to rise as resources for welfare declined.
Where growth was permitted for social workers it increasingly carried with
it the social policing condition. In comparison with other possible child-care

initiatives this was relatively cheap precisely because it was seen as *an individual reactive service*.

Because this account concerns state social work it does give a one-sided picture. Throughout the 1970s and the 1980s, voluntary child-care agencies made use of their greater freedom to explore alternative, often preventive approaches to child care (see for example Goldberg, 1987; Holman, 1988; Gibbons, 1990). However, it is interesting that the voluntary agency which experienced the most publicity and the greatest growth, the NSPCC, has mainly focused on reactive work in child abuse (Cooper 1987, ch. 2).

This brief history should reveal at least the overall pressures on, and major movements within child care social work in the last twenty years. It might be argued that this period has been turbulent for *all* welfare workers and agencies but the semi-professional base and the social science influences have created particular difficulties for social workers at a time of reducing services and higher public alarms. The present state of social work will be considered fully at the end of the chapter but, before that, we shall analyse the important matter of social work education and training.

Training, elitism, egalitarianism and the managers

A simple view of training is that it makes people better at their jobs and that it provides a reference point for anyone who is interested in what that job involves – clients, the public, the state and the workers themselves. If such a training acquires some kind of official validation it can also be viewed as a minimum for a particular kind of work, distinguishing between those who have done the training and those who have not. However the fact that this *is* a simple view means that it is unlikely to explain the position of social workers! Even the term 'training' is suspect, as seen by the fact that the body overseeing such matters in social work is named the Central Council for *Education and Training* in Social Work (CCETSW) (italics added).

Professionalism – to be or not to be

The coming of social services departments in 1971 brought with it the need for a new generic form of training and the two-year Certificate of Qualification in Social Work (CQSW) was quickly introduced (reduced to one year for certain graduates). However, despite fast expansion, there was a serious shortage of qualified staff during the early 1970s. In addition a large number of staff especially in SSDS were concerned with work that related to but was different from the existing definition of (mainly field) social work. As a result and with the active support of employers a separate qualification was introduced, the Certificate of Social Service (CSS). Whatever the delicate language of the time it was evident that, in terms of salary and promotion the CQSW was more valuable than the CSS.

The British Association of Social Workers (BASW) fully supported the introduction of the CSS in 1975 but within a short time was expressing great alarm about a CCETSW proposal to equate the two qualifications (see Sibeon, 1991, pp. 33 and 36–38). Yet within this period BASW itself, at a historic annual general meeting in 1979, voted for open membership; this meant that anyone occupying what could be designated a social work post was henceforth eligible to join the association. (This decision, incidentally, still influences the BASW position in relation to current discussions over the possible establishment of a national social work (or services) council.) Nevertheless employers now normally expect that field social work posts will be restricted to holders of the CQSW but this, of course, also includes CSS holders.

These training developments highlight the three factors in the title of this section. During the 1970s the growth of 'radical social work' brought with it a demand for a more egalitarian stance from social work. Put simply, social workers were criticized as distancing themselves from their clients, as elitist and as part of the professionalization process analysed by Illich (1973) and others. Their CQSW qualification symbolized this distance and thus needed to be kept under control. As an attender of the 1979 BASW Annual General Meeting, the author recalls the sincerity and ambivalence of the debates. The final vote for open membership, though far from unanimous, seemed to represent a mixture of political conviction, moral compassion and guilt – a blend which continues to characterize social work.

Thus the twin conflicting aims of professional improvement and egalitarianism have long been evident in social work and, as we shall see later, they are key ingredients in the debate about the future. However, the third factor of 'the managers' also requires discussion. As we indicated, social work employers were anxious to train their staff and for those who could not undertake the CQSW for whatever reason the new CSS was developed as an agency-run, in-house system. This increasing employer involvement and expertise in training later put pressure on the college-based CQSW.

More importantly, it illustrated a growing gap between academics and senior agency staff and this was reflected in the essential differences between the two forms of training. While CQSW intakes were full-time, national, strongly based on the broad social sciences and generic, CSS schemes trained their own local staff (although most schemes were consortia of several agencies) within their host agency on a job-release basis, emphasized skill development and allowed for specialisms. The growing power of employers was reflected in the next important development in social work training.

Three years: the irreducible minimum and its reduction

In July 1986 CCETSW issued Paper 20.6. This set out clear proposals for a new *three year* training programme for social work to replace the CQSW and CSS qualifications and to be called the Qualifying Diploma in Social Work (QDSW). In bold language CCETSW nailed its minimum colours to the mast and after quoting favourable comment from the Beckford Inquiry Report said:

> In both educational and practical terms it is impossible to produce in two years a qualified social worker able to operate competently, effectively, and with some degree of special knowledge. The minimum period for qualification must be three years. (CCETSW, 1986, p. 5)

The new training, reducible to two years for graduates with relevant experience, would for the first time require joint planning, design and management by alliances of employers and colleges. It would be full- or part-time and for at least one year (but not necessarily more) students would be registered at a college. As well:

> All students must undertake at least one period of supervised assessed practice outside their normal place of work (this could, however, be within the student's employing agency). (ibid., p. 16)

The influence of CSS and the employers is very evident here. There was some alarm amongst academics that employed students would have a restricted experience if they were confined to their own agencies for practice placements but this battle was lost. CCETSW did, however, refuse an earlier proposal that the placement could be within the student's workplace. There were also doubts about the joint ownership of courses (see Pinker, 1986) as a real threat to academic freedom. At the same time the three year proposal was universally welcomed so compromise on other issues was always likely.

Within a year the entire scheme was in ruins. The Conservative Government which had done nothing to contradict the consensus from child abuse inquiries that social workers needed to improve their practice, flatly rejected CCETSW's proposals. Instead, the Government insisted that in future the two-year period should provide not just basic generic training but also expertise in particular fields.

For historians and sociologists, the failure of social work to marshal any cohesive or forceful protest against this decision deserves study. For all the bad publicity surrounding child abuse, social workers were on the child-care agenda and the public was beginning to acknowledge the complexity of the social work role. Although the Beckford and Carlyle Reports were particularly critical it seems feasible to argue that with the right kind of campaign a very strong case could have been made that better training would improve protection.

A further factor was the European Community. In anticipation of the free movement of labour after 1992 a project was commissioned to draw up an 'approved list' of professional qualifications used by member countries (see Barr, 1990). UK training was conspicuously excluded from this list, accompanied only by Denmark and in the case of the latter the objections were mainly technical. The EC's reasons for the exclusion were first that UK social work had no regulatory body and secondly that its training was less than three years. Within the UK itself it was noticeable that social workers' most frequent collaborators, health visitors, nurses, occupational therapists and teachers, all trained for longer periods.

Perhaps no amount of resistance by social workers would have influenced an extremely hostile government which had in 1987 just been re-elected. Nevertheless, the lack of *concerted* effective opposition via CCETSW and BASW is a serious indictment. The reasons may lie in the increasing divisions within social work itself. Bearing in mind the view of social work as essentially definable in terms of its work/employer setting we can refer to Howe's (1991) assessment of where power now lies. Quoting Friedson, Howe suggests that within any profession are found three types of member – practitioners, administrators and teacher–researchers (pp. 205–8) – and goes on to argue that power has increasingly shifted towards administrators who, of course, include managers. However this does not explain, per se, the three-year training issue because surely managers would be as keen as anyone to have a well-trained workforce. This apparent paradox will be explored in the next section as will the other equally difficult question: why were practitioners themselves so evidently unsuccessful in fighting for the longer training?

Whatever the reasons UK social work training remains too short compared with that of other similar groups within this country and within Europe. At the time of writing CQSW and CSS courses are being replaced by the two-year Diploma in Social Work (DipSW). This has incorporated many of the valuable principles of the abortive QDSW proposals: collaborative planning leading to joint ownership by colleges and agencies, increased linkage between theory and practice and improved training of agency placement supervisors (practice teachers). For all the earlier criticisms of the CQSW it was, ironically, in the area of placements that the greatest weakness may have lain. The involvement of employers in the new training should ensure that this issue receives more attention. Even so, many agencies, especially social services departments, are under-resourced and at present, the provision of good placements remains difficult especially in large urban areas.

The future of training remains uncertain. The obvious limitations of two years can be reduced by the development of advanced training, known as post-qualifying (PQ); however this important area remains under discussion with neither aims nor strategies yet agreed; even more important, government funding levels and arrangements for PQ are far from certain.

Although there has been a general welcome within social work for closer employer/college collaboration in training it is important to consider the wider political context. The present government has shown a strong general preference for on-the-job, employer dominated forms of training. This was evident in the White Paper *Employment for the 1990s* (Department of Employment, 1988) with its proposal to reform youth training in order to 'give the leadership of the training schemes to employers where it belongs' (p. 43). Similarly, current government proposals seek to increase the amount of time that trainee teachers spend in schools and this is provoking strong opposition from colleges and teachers' trade unions. Although this philosophy may have attractions for social work employers as meeting their immediate needs it has implications for the longer term integrity and independence of social work training.

There is not space here to tackle the ultimate question of *what* training will be offered in social work. The earlier preference, dating from Seebohm times, for a generic model covering all client groups, work settings and methods of working is now being eroded. Increasingly in the workplace, social workers are specializing with the main division being between child care on the one hand and work with adults on the other, overlaid with new methods of dividing up all the work into either 'purchase', which includes assessment and the negotiation of services, or 'provision', which refers to the delivery of various forms of services to clients and consumers. The very fact that both 'clients' and 'consumers' are used in social work terminology indicates the co-existence of different views of what should be done and how.

Because of the major political changes that have taken place in the UK in the last thirteen years social work, like all welfare sectors, is in a state of flux. Training will inevitably reflect that but it will also be affected by other important influences and it is these that will be discussed next in assessing the development of social work in child care.

Influences within social work

As suggested in Chapter 1, it would be too convenient to picture social work as a well-meaning activity that has merely been put at the mercy of outsiders. That would neglect the wide areas of discretion within which its members have influenced their own fate. So we should also retain the three-fold division outlined by Howe, of practitioners, administrators and teacher–researchers, for it is argued here that they have different influences on social work. We also propose another important distinction: between the *embracing of global goals* and the *pursuit of professional improvement*.

Managerialism

The previous two sections of this chapter referred to the growth of social services departments and the influence of managers. In the early 1970s there was considerable debate about how professional practitioners should or could fit into large bureaucracies (Glastonbury, et al. 1982). An important influence at that time was the work of the Brunel Institute of Organisation and Social Studies (Social Services Organisation Research Unit) (BIOSS, 1974) and their clear assumption that practitioners would have, not so much autonomy, as 'delegated discretion'. As departments grew in size so their functions became more complex and managers found their interests and allegiances diverting more and more from front-line issues (see Bamford, 1982; Howe, 1986).

Recent political pressures to reduce the direct state provision of services, the growth of privatization and the need to control costs have brought further dilemmas for managers. Qualified social workers form only part of social services department staff, perhaps as little as 10 per cent, and this has obviously affected thinking. In addition, there is an increasing tendency to appoint managers without social work qualifications for the perfectly sound reason that they might well make good managers. Thus, as the managerial role has changed so has the perception of social workers; this is a long way from, for example, the setting up of Children's Departments in 1948 when the chief officer was seen as having a *personal* responsibility over all the children looked after by the new service.

This inevitable division between managers and practitioners may help to explain the failure of the QDSW in the last section. It could be argued that social services managers' first priority (and understandably so) was not to improve *social work* training but to establish a basic *social services* training especially in under-developed areas such as day-care and residential care. If so then, politically, their task may have seemed easier if they accepted the hostile line of the Government in 1987.

The managerial task has since become even more complex with the coming of government proposals for care in the community. A White Paper in 1988 followed by an Act in 1990 with initial plans for implementation in April 1992 (since postponed for a year) have created enormous demands on social services managers. The changes required by the legislation will totally reshape budgets, deeply rooted methods of service delivery and organization. Unlike 1971 there is no safe assumption about the central role for social work within social services provision except in the areas of child protection and mental health. Services for children and families seem destined to have an important social work element but only in the care management sector. The philosophy of a mixed economy of welfare will assume that services in this area could be bought from a wide range of providers with no *guaranteed* place for social work practitioners. Even within child protection there seems a clear preference for regulated procedures which are more amenable to management monitoring.

The influence of a management view can also be seen in the relatively muted challenge to the concept of care in the community as currently defined. One fundamental effect might be to reduce rights by converting *claimants* (those who have been *eligible* for social security benefits because they are in residential care) into social services *clients*, dependent on discretionary assessments (Sapey, 1992). This criticism echoes that made by Jordan (1974) in his analysis of the use of discretionary payments by social workers. Perhaps with a growing (but inevitable?) sense that the Government proposals were unstoppable managerial concerns have become increasingly pragmatic: Is there any money? Is there enough time to plan? rather than, Is the principle to be challenged?

Events of the last few years have strengthened the relative role of social services managers. Their functions have been endorsed by the government, but only at a price: that they behave in a way compatible with a market view of welfare. Although child care may ultimately be less affected than other service areas some of its strongest traditions of protection allied with caring, work through personal relationships and wide areas of worker discretion, face major challenges.

Teacher–researchers

Child care has had a long tradition of sound, sometimes unsung, empirical research, through workers such as Beveridge, the Dartington Social Research Unit, Holman, Packman, Parker, Rowe, Stevenson and Thoburn. Since the mid-1980s the influence of these and others seems to have been better acknowledged. An important government sponsored publication (DHSS, 1985) provided a landmark summary of recent child-care research into social work around the care experience.

The planning surrounding the 1989 Children Act also re-affirmed the importance of research findings and Parton (1991, ch. 7) identifies the extent of professional lobbying. Thus:

> While the Government was clearly not keen to change *the structure and philosophy of the legislation*, the lobby groups were particularly active to refine it in certain respects. (p. 192; italics added)

One of the most impressive features of the Act has been the wealth of good quality training material commissioned by the Department of Health from sources such as the Open University, Family Rights Group, Leicester University and the National Children's Bureau. The 1985 publication was also re-echoed to some extent by an important summary of research into child-care placements (DoH, 1991e).

These writings were further enhanced by contributions from writers in the field of anti-discrimination, an element which had been lacking or at best restricted in earlier works. Key contributors have been Dominelli (1988 and 1989), Ahmed et al. (1986), and Ahmad (1989). Although the research base of these writers has been limited they have had an increasing influence on other child-care theorists and this is something that will be further explored in the next section.

Thus there has been a continuing tradition of *systematic* study and research which has had influence on social work. However, the majority of the research has been restricted to child-care *practice*. Once we move into the realms of child abuse and its causes this picture of careful, relatively neutral research is much less applicable. The major influences on social workers have come from elsewhere and their soundness is far less certain. Objectivity has been weakened by assertions and strong value positions in a field characterized by constantly changing definitions and ideological battles. As a result, we suggest that the government has been much more open to traditional mainstream child-care practice research than to other contributions. What are these other areas?

Practitioners and anti-discrimination

For all the importance of the mainstream work identified in the last section, how influential has it been? The Beckford Report was extremely critical of social workers' lack of knowledge and skills and, despite its simplistic view of child protection, it touched a raw nerve. Relative to other professions, social work has not enjoyed a good reputation for intellectual rigour. Serious academic journals are not widely read by practitioners. Especially in the state sector, research by practitioners is infrequent and the system of post-qualifying training has been persistently under-funded and underdeveloped. If the commendable investment in the Children Act in training materials marks a change in this picture it will be an important watershed. Nevertheless, one of the most dramatic influences on practitioners in child care may have come from elsewhere.

Since the mid-1980s two major 'ISMS,' anti-racism and anti-sexism have had an enormous impact on social work as the major themes of anti-discrimination. Of these the latter has been especially significant in child abuse thinking and practice. They are included in this section on practitioners rather than teacher-researchers because as indicated before, their formal research base *within the field of social work practice* is not sufficient to explain their influence.

Essentially these 'isms' are *global themes* in that they make radical critiques of the nature of modern society. As Williams (1989, chs 3 and 4) demonstrates, they have forced fundamental reviews of previous social-reformist and Marxist thinking. Their theorizing has been powerful in explanatory terms although anti-racist writings still have difficulty in separating race from class and poverty as a *specific* contributor to child-care issues. Bebbington and Miles (1989) in a study of the background of children who enter local authority care (2500 children in a cross-section of local authorities) do not find, overall, that children from ethnic minorities are over-represented. Similarly, the emotive question of trans-racial adoption remains badly under-researched. Anti-sexism has been in a more powerful position because evidence of male violence and sexual abuse both to women and to children (Dominelli, 1989) cannot easily be explained in simple socio-economic terms.

Anti-racism and anti-sexism are primarily concerned with attitudes. Ahmad (1989) makes clear that further research into child care is not, per se, enough and says:

> In Britain nearly all research work on black children and young people has common characteristics. Researchers are predominantly white and their approaches Eurocentric. (p. 152)

Their approach is clearly so fundamental in terms of social policy that it has come to acquire the status of a moral and political movement. The evidence for this view is in the style and language of much of the literature. 'Challenge' 'confront' and 'combat' are terms not often found in traditional child care literature, especially since the 1970s.

Anti-racism's first major appearance came through a 'mass lobby' by the Mickleton Group outside a CCETSW council meeting in December 1986 to demand an end to 'overwhelmingly racist' policies in social work (*Social Work Today*, 15/12/86, p. 3). This dramatic tactic set the pattern for lobbying which has been very effective if we look at CCETSW's current position. Paper 30 (1989) which lays down requirements for DipSW training requires that it be underpinned in 'every aspect' by anti-discrimination.

How is this influence to be assessed? In the next chapter we shall consider what kinds of child abuse knowledge are available and useful to social workers. At this stage it is enough to acknowledge that the fundamental arguments of anti-racism and anti-sexism have made important contributions. Feminist analyses have forced often uncomfortable re-assessments of child abuse and brought previously shadowy areas into the light, particularly in the matter of women as victims rather than as colluders. Their challenges to family dysfunction theorists have opened up valuable new ways of assessing parent–child relationships. Anti-racism has cast serious doubts on a traditional colour-blind liberalism that was very common in social work and has encouraged a more positive approach to developing the resources of black communities. It might also be said that socialism will never be the same again because of these two critiques.

Despite these benefits the influence of the major 'isms' has also been problematic for social work for three reasons, one theoretical, one psychological and one strategic.

Jordan (1991) makes the important point that the anti-discrimination requirements set out by CCETSW for DipSW training represent a value position that clashes with an older position in social work deriving from a *liberal* respect for rights and the protection of individuals. Anti-discrimination as expressed in current thinking requires a much more challenging intrusive stance which argues that racism and sexism are sins of omission as much as commission. This is not only a theoretical problem but also a practical one and Jordan is critical of CCETSW for simply placing these conflicting values side-by-side in Paper 30 without comment.

Jordan sees anti-discrimination as part of a wider structural concern but this view does not adequately distinguish between the current anti-discrimination movement and the earlier 1970s interest in class and poverty. Unlike the latter, anti-discrimination has created much more tension within social work because of its less compromising stance. It is here that the *psychological* issue arises. We might speculate that the poverty problem is an ultimately insoluble dilemma for mostly middle-class social workers: during the day they confront their clients' lack of money and then return, in the main, to a much more comfortable existence. With anti-sexism and even more so anti-racism the *private* attitudes of the worker or teacher are more visible through his/her daily lifestyle and language interactions. Is it possible that some of the fervour of anti-discrimination is an expiation of the guilt felt by social workers at their previous failure to make much impact on their clients' poverty? The psychology here is complex but the current tensions within social work are evident.

Since 1986 there has been a new mood of challenge and confrontation, of allegation and censure. Weekly social work journals record serious disputes within agencies and colleges that ring with accusation and denial. It is no exaggeration to say that, particularly for training colleges, an allegation of racism or sexism can have very serious consequences. Can we detect an aura, almost of fear of something which Webb (1990–1) has labelled a new 'puritanism'? This is characterized by a moral certainty and a narrow orthodoxy that prescribes acceptable behaviour and is quick to condemn deviations.

Because of the theoretical paradox described by Jordan it is likely that individuals within some social work may well experience some confusion and conflict and this is very stressful. Puritanism cannot easily adjust to such a situation, because, as anti-discrimination in its extreme form it rightly sees the need for determination and single-mindedness if it is to achieve a more equitable society. But this provokes clashes with the more traditional and still valuable liberal position of tolerance for individual differences.

We identified a third problem as strategic or perhaps even pragmatic. The debates regarding anti-discrimination have been largely *within* social work, a kind of internal battle for the moral high ground. Yet during the same period the record of challenges against other external threats to clients has been less vigorous and less successful. We have already mentioned the submissiveness of social work in the face of the government's refusal to allow a three-year training course. The Social Fund, growing family poverty and now care in the community all represent profound dangers to clients yet social work has an unimpressive record of cohesive or coherent public protest. In an era when *all* providers of health and social welfare have had to fight for survival, social work has been largely absent from television screens and newspapers. It has not been seen either by the public or the Government as an authentic and expert source of comment on major social issues affecting children, and this is a sad state of affairs. Again, does this bear out my suspicion that the 'isms' partly stem from social workers' frustration and guilt about their impotence in other even more fundamental areas?

It is thus essential to distinguish between the central importance to social work of an anti-discrimination base and the extent and method of its promotion which should be a matter of open and reasoned debate. This should include what might seem a further paradox. Because anti-discrimination is global in its application, its proponents have not limited their challenges to the here and now and so to the present Government! Thus Corby's (1991) interesting observation that

> on the face of it, one could cynically argue that the feminist perspective and the state's needs have temporarily been in agreement, despite the fact that their analyses of the problem are vastly different. The radical feminist perspective sees child sexual abuse as an outcome of male-dominated and male-orientated structures and as a problem to be firmly tackled in the face of expected resistance from *all* quarters [my italics]. It does not link the issue to class and poverty. (p. 101)

This is borne out by the observation that anti-discrimination was not noticeably on the agenda in the 1992 General Election campaign, whereas poverty clearly was.

Party politics is increasingly about short-term visible issues, so on this basis the anti-discrimination movement in social work has not threatened the present government. Rather they, and others, have been able to agree with it in principle but also represent it as yet another internal social work squabble. The media reaction to the 1991 BASW Annual General Meeting illustrates this very well. The meeting featured allegations of discrimination by some participants against others and this received much more publicity in the local press than any of the other important issues debated there.

This analysis raises awkward questions. On moral grounds anti-discrimination is unchallengeable. Social workers, despite what internal critics say, have largely accepted this view and begun to underpin their practice accordingly. The debate therefore needs to address the conceptual, psychological and strategic problems identified earlier. Is it possible to retain the commitment and energy of the anti-discrimination movement and tune it productively to the special nature of social work and its distinctive functions? If this is to happen it needs to be acknowledged that there are limits to the social work sphere and that it is not simply a *background* to radical politics.

The future of social work

Child-care work in the last twenty years has exaggerated the formal agency base as the means of defining social work. A public and political wish to emphasize child protection has correspondingly reduced other areas of work. To some extent social workers themselves have welcomed this trend partly because it was a compensation for the lost battles of the 1960s and 1970s for a radical approach to child-care problems. It also offered the attractions of more specialist work, but this differed in important respects from the earlier children's service of the 1950s and 1960s. The public and political mood had changed and economic expansion was at an end. The new specialism was more lightly regulated, less successful in the eyes of the public and finally more focused on control than on promotion.

On the other hand, social work has regained a degree of radicalness through the influence of anti-discrimination which provides value bases *additional* to existing concerns about class and poverty and about liberal respect for individual dignity. The agency-base analysis of social work is persuasive and probably well founded but it does not do justice to a deep-rooted concern with fundamental values and distinctive ways of working. This is why training for social work is crucial and has been discussed at some length. If it merely prepares social workers to fit into the major agencies and carry out their requirements it may sell short the values base. Jordan in his recent writing (1990) has been keen to redefine social work within ethical frameworks and this will be essential if practitioners are to have a solid foundation for their work; but as we indicated above, where different value positions co-exist they need to be synthesized in training courses.

For child abuse the issues are important. Social workers who are simply agents of protection agencies may find it more difficult to operate beyond official procedures and guidelines arising from legislation, more difficult to use professional discretion in taking risks. Child abuse work is rarely simple and as we shall argue in the next chapter, the knowledge base is far from firm; all the more reason that well-trained workers should seek the freedom to roam widely in their search for approaches and methods that promote as well as protect children's welfare. This is likely to require styles of work that move in and out of the statutory boundaries and are open to more informal sources of help.

The current developments towards care in the community will have a major impact on who social workers will be, what they will do, where and how. If the economic recession continues it seems likely that social work roles and tasks may be reduced, with more work taken over by less qualified or by the voluntary and private sector. This may leave child protection as the core of child-care work or even, at worst, the sum of it. On the other hand, it may herald the movement of many social workers into positions outside the statutory services. If so a clear well-founded identity will become even more essential if social work is not to fragment into constituent parts as therapist, counsellor, community organiser or substitute care provider. From children's point of view the fact that social work is such a huge mix of functions and activities brings benefits; a wide view is possible of children's needs ranging from prevention, through promotion and protection on to caring and after-care.

The future brings threats to work in the child abuse field but it may also offer some exciting challenges. To meet these challenges social work needs more than ever the ability and will to evaluate its position, to clarify its value bases and practically, to establish the range of its social mandate – what can be done and what is beyond it.

Summary

Social work stands at the point where the family meets the State in time of trouble and for this reason it is important to children. It also has features of a semi-profession pitched into public gaze in the last twenty years and its development is of intrinsic interest.

We have reiterated the way child protection has come to be the dominant part of child care work and the recent history has been explored. Developments in training have been central to understanding the position of social work and we consider that the present position is unsatisfactory. As well as external factors there have been important internal influences during this period and these indicate that social work is not a unitary or unified activity. Managers have had an increasing and distinctive influence on practice as has the anti-discrimination movement. Both of these have posed major value and practice issues for social work and merit further study.

Because of the major changes ahead, through care in the community legislation and restructuring, crucial challenges again face social workers and their work in child abuse will be greatly affected. Whatever else happens that work is best done on the basis of systematic knowledge and we turn to this issue in the next chapter.

4/ KNOWLEDGE

Definitions, statistics and assumptions

What do we know?

Seeking knowledge about child abuse has four functions: establishing definitions, agreeing significance and measuring prevalence, discovering causes, and developing ways of preventing or reducing it.

The arrangement of this list is not accidental for it has both a historical and an intellectual logic. In modern times, until something ultimately called child abuse was identified the process of doing something about it could not begin. This may seem obvious but the essential point is that the definition defines the consequences and as we have indicated earlier the recent history of child abuse has been complicated. Child battering, non-accidental injury, physical abuse, neglect, emotional abuse, sexual abuse, system abuse and most recently, ritual abuse, are all terms which have been used both theoretically and empirically by researchers and practitioners in the field.

Cooper and Ball (1987, ch. 1) compare and contrast the modern 'discovery' of child abuse with that of AIDS and suggest that the former has suffered far greater difficulties of definition than the latter and with corresponding problems in treatment. This book contributes to the definition debate, and no doubt complicates it, by adopting a deliberately wide view of the phenomenon. Others may prefer a narrower concept and clearly both views raise problems because they will then determine how significant and prevalent child abuse is. Both terms are important in human life because we may decide to invest time and resources in something which although very uncommon, is so distressing that it seems justified; thus there are extremely rare childhood diseases that we may nevertheless want to tackle with great energy. Alternatively, the sheer scale of a problem will give it a social momentum and perhaps unemployment has now come into this category.

In the earlier chapter on law it might have been commented that debates about emergency protection have consumed energy which is disproportionate to the small number of children who need it. Yet, because of the importance of emergency protection in terms of personal rights, the effort is justified. Definitions of child abuse need to be considered in these terms so that intrinsic significance is continually balanced against sheer frequency. This book's stance is that forms of abuse, such as neglect and developmental damage caused by social factors, are widespread and that they have received less attention in recent years from social work theorists and policy-makers than they deserve.

Because the definition of child abuse has been so difficult to achieve, measuring prevalence (and incidence too) is complex. Taylor (1989, ch. 3) explores these problems and argues, for example, that in one of the most widely publicized surveys of sexual abuse (the MORI Poll, see Baker and Duncan, 1986) the definition offered to adult respondents was:

> a minefield of ambiguity, including terms such as 'sexually mature', 'erotic arousal', 'touching', 'pornographic material', and 'talking about things in an erotic way'. In fact, it is almost a textbook example of how *not* to write a survey question. (p. 49)

Birchall, too, in a well-documented review (1989) summarizes child abuse definitions and frequency within the UK and the USA. For the United States she says:

> Gil and Noble derived from the three per cent figure an incidence of 2.5–4 million physical injuries per annum, a rate of 13–21 per 1000 children. They compared this estimate with national register totals, then averaging 6,300 per annum. Even allowing for the probability that the registers will miss the more minor injuries, this discrepancy is staggering! (p. 12)

and later, in considering sexual abuse in the USA, she refers to reported rates that ranged from 6 to 62 per cent for girls and 3 to 20 per cent for boys (p. 21). The USA experiences are relevant because, first, research has been more numerous there, and second, it is clear that, to date, the UK has closely followed American thinking.

A curious feature of the UK scene is that, despite its public concern about child abuse the Government has only recently begun to collect national statistics (Department of Health since 1988). These derive from the collation of returns from local authorities of children on child protection registers and therefore measure official concern rather than incidence. Even here, the data is of limited value (see Walton, 1989, ch. 10).

Within sexual abuse the problem of definition and measurement seems particularly acute. The phenomenon has many of the features of a 'moral panic', showing lurid media publicity, contagious alarm and an exponential growth in concern and reported influence since its initial inclusion in official registers in 1981. The frequently used current definition, drawn from Schechter and Roberge (1976) is extremely wide and this needs to be treated with caution, yet it is all too common to hear not only members of the public but also social work practitioners using the term casually to cover anything from persistent buggery to isolated incidents with 'flashers' in public parks. Recent research by Kelly et al. (1991) is a creditable attempt to address some of these definition issues in a retrospective study. A continuing problem, however, is to establish whether assessments of sexual (and other forms of) abuse incidents are based on a on a view of their *inherent wrongness* or of their *consequences* for the victims.

Because child abuse is by definition an emotive subject, striking at the heart of personal and family life it has become an analyst's nightmare. All too often it has been an ideological and political battlefield where systematic and rational research have been pushed to the sidelines. The government's belated entry into the assessment of child abuse is welcome but elsewhere it has preferred to rely on individual case inquiries whose brief has been too limited to provide any general information. Should we now be pressing for a wide-ranging Royal Commission into children's suffering?

Causes of abuse

There is no shortage of literature on the causes of child abuse. A summary, of the major theoretical approaches is available in Corby (1989, ch. 2) and Browne (1988, ch. 2) and a brief review of the main causal models for sexual abuse in Pringle (1990), while O'Hagan (1989) discusses feminist and family dysfunction perspectives in sexual abuse (ch. 3). Structural factors which may affect families are explored in Holman (1988), Goldberg (1987) and Garbarino and Gillam (1980) while Alloway and Bebbington (1987) review literature relating to the 'buffer' influence of family support. De'ath (1989, ch. 3) also provides a wide review of the present state of the family and the pressures on it.

What is available and what influences practice are not the same. Earlier chapters have charted the way social work in child abuse has moved through the 1980s. Parton (1991) in analysing the trend says:

> It is perhaps ironic that one of the net outcomes of all the criticisms directed at social workers and others to fulfil their responsibilities to protect children appropriately was to confirm and contrast child protection as *the* central responsibility for social work. Thus, rather than being simply one of the range of child care services and skills that social services departments offered, it became the main priority. (p. 204)

As Parton also argues, this protection of children was against *individuals* – in most cases their parents. For this reason social workers have drawn much more heavily on literature about individual causes of child abuse, the 'disease model', than on structural approaches, and this may partly explain Davies' (1991) argument that sociology appears to have had little real impact because:

> Macro-perspectives, by their very nature, exclude the interests of individuals; indeed the very idea of 'individualism' is often presented as methodologically unsound. But the world of social work – like the intimate world of ordinary men and women – is almost wholly taken up with the lives and fortunes of individuals. (p. 6)

Any themes which seemed to offer information about why *individuals* might abuse children were generally welcomed by social workers and practice aids have reflected this. The Government publication *Protecting Children* (DoH, 1988) is widely distributed in social services departments but McBeath and Webb (1990–91) argue that it is shakily based on a view of individual rights and responsibilities which appear to be set in a theoretical and social vacuum. They also question the authoritative line of this document and suggest that: 'low-level theoretical language pervades social work literature to create an atmosphere of specialist objective, rational knowledge' (p. 140).

The idea of abuse indicator checklists is obviously an attractive one to practitioners and the Beckford Report was apparently confident that such things existed if only social workers would go out and read them. However the problems of *prediction* of, and screening for, child abuse have been extensively discussed (Starr, 1982; Browne et al., 1988). Dingwall (1989) also reviews the field and concludes:

> In terms of Blom-Cooper's [chairman of the Beckford Inquiry] challenge, though, this paper must come to a bleak conclusion. The amount of scientifically validated research on child abuse and neglect is vanishingly small. The value of any self-styled predictive checklist is negligible. (p. 51)

None of this means that the causes of child abuse are unknowable. What it does suggest is that social work is not in a position to follow convenient guidelines and procedures in assessing individual situations. Furthermore, if those guidelines focus too narrowly on the disease model they are bound to be incomplete and likely to encourage a biased approach to decision-making.

Feminism as knowledge

If, as Davies suggests, social workers have preferred individual psychology to sociology in dealing with child abuse, how do we explain the considerable impact of feminism on current thinking? Any theory which promotes the rights of around half the population can hardly be considered an 'individual' approach yet it has received wide publicity in social work literature, although its effect on practice is more difficult to estimate.

We began this chapter by suggesting four functions of knowledge about child abuse and it is instructive to apply these to feminism.

First, regarding *definitions* the impact has been enormous. Thus feminist writers have challenged traditional narrow views of incest and rape with some success. While the 1984 Criminal Law Revision Committee concluded (by majority decision) that immunity from rape allegations should remain within marriage, by 1990 a Law Commission Paper *Rape Within Marriage* forcefully rejected the earlier arguments (Hoggett and Pearl, 1991, pp. 38–42) and a very recent court ruling seems to have established clearly that rape is rape wherever it takes place.

Influential literature ranging from Erin Pizzey's sharply titled *Scream Quietly or the Neighbours Will Hear* (1974) through to more theoretical works (Dobash and Dobash, 1980) and empirical studies (Pahl, 1985) combined with compelling statistics about wife battering and child sexual abuse have forced major changes in UK attitudes. Although radical feminists see the gains as modest compared with what remains to be done there is no doubt that the *way* we think is changing.

In the matter of prevalence of child abuse, feminism encounters the same problems as any other perspective – the lack of sound and reliable research. The danger of a movement which is seeking fundamental social change is that in challenging past underestimates of abuse it may go too far the other way. Thus a comment such as 'we know that *all* women and girls in our society have experienced or are experiencing some kind of sexual assault in our day-to-day lives' (Manning, 1988, p. 22; italics added) is a political rather than an empirical assertion. Similarly, the notion that *all* men are potential rapists is of limited practical value to a busy social worker although in definitional terms it is an important statement.

The third and fourth functions of knowledge, to suggest causes and to propose methods of prevention or reducing abuse, can be considered together. If, as feminism argues, much violence arises from deeply entrenched patriarchy then both women and children (as well of course, as men themselves) are victims of a structural problem. Any reduction in abuse would thus require radical long-term social changes. Many of these are far beyond the role and capacity of social work; employment policy would be a major example.

The working female is a key element in understanding the position of women as mothers. The number of married women working has gone from around 50 per cent to over 70 per cent between 1971 and 1989 (Central Statistical Office, 1991). From one point of view this is a welcome move towards an escape from the kitchen sink, but a closer analysis suggests that this freedom has a heavy cost (see Hudson and Lee, 1990). Women continue to occupy a disproportionate share of lower paid jobs, may be less well paid than before when they return to work after childbirth, are likely to do more than their fair share of housework while holding down a job, and show higher levels of stress. On the other hand, the period when mothers are *not* working after childbirth is smaller than before (Hoggett and Pearl, 1991, p. 79). This may mean in future that women will have a greater negotiating power in relation to employment if only because they will have longer to make an impact. In the shorter term a feminist analysis would see mothers occupying three possible disadvantaged positions: first, as mothers at home, if they are lone parents they are likely to suffer poverty; secondly, if they have male partners they are also likely to experience some form of personal oppression; thirdly, if they are working they are likely to be earning poor wages while continuing to have child-care responsibilities. Of these possible situations the position of lone parents is especially important for children. Bebbington and Miles (1989) in their study of 2500 children coming into care in thirteen local authorities found that living in a single-parent household was the most significant associated factor increasing the likelihood of admission to care by eight times.

The presence of a male partner is obviously problematic in feminist terms. Finkelhor's identification of the step-father as 'the strongest correlate' for sexual abuse of children (see Glaser and Frosh, 1988, pp. 14–15) and the general evidence that men commit the great majority of sexual abuse all support a feminist explanation. However, because feminism has to adopt a global stance to maintain its explanatory power it has to use *deductive* methods to explain particular circumstances. Thus where a man or woman cohabit and no child abuse is *evident* feminism may be tempted to argue that it hasn't yet been detected, or it may resort to something like the following selective explanation:

> The argument presented above should not be taken to mean that there is no difference between a family in which abuse occurs and one in which it does not. If it is correct that the *potential* for abuse resides in all families and all men, then what differentiates the two groups of factors is the power of inhibiting factors. *The most important of these may well be the behaviour of the mother'*. (Glaser and Frosh, 1988, pp. 44; italics added)

This illustrates the tendency of any theory to make the facts fit; it also threatens the kind of systematic family assessment called for in documents such as *Protecting Children*. By eliminating from the equation, possible change in the *father* it restricts intervention strategies. If a causal model moves too readily and whimsically between a general background account (the position of women in general) and a particular foreground explanation (the plight of this mother here and now at the hands of a male partner) it value is reduced.

The power dimension

Power is central to the feminist position. It is seen as residing historically in men and the thrust is to reduce this inequality. However this does not directly address two issues. First, the children's rights movement (see Chapter 2) is concerned with the power imbalance between children and *adults* rather than just men. Where this imbalance results in child abuse, social workers may take court action and this often on the basis of the mother's behaviour. Dominelli and McLeod (1989) accept this is a 'blind spot' (p. 72) for feminist theorists and workers but argue that where mothers ill-treat their children it is because 'they are reinforcing the patriarchal principle that force legitimately underwrites hierarchical relations' (ibid., p. 89). It is suggested in subsequent pages that somehow a less patriarchal society would also be less violent towards its children.

The Cleveland affair is instructive here. Campbell (1988 and 1991) analysed the events in terms of a male establishment and the MP Stuart Bell and the police in particular, acting to suppress and vilify a feminist inspired attempt to bring the full extent of sexual abuse to public attention. While some elements of the affair support this view Campbell seems to have overlooked the even more fundamental question of *professional power over children*. The Inquiry team, (headed by a woman judge) were, in the end, not questioning the paediatricians' diagnoses; rather they criticized the apparent lack of awareness and sensitivity about what those diagnoses led to – a drastic legalistic process that diminished children and parents as individuals with a right to participate in and be consulted about what was happening to them.

In this way feminism runs a risk that its causal base can hamper good practice. A concern to rescue women and children from abuse by men has been a strong feature of the movement particularly in areas of domestic violence. When this is translated into child protection, as appeared to happen in Cleveland, other considerations were seen less clearly. Dominelli and McLeod (1989) acknowledge this dilemma saying: 'In keeping with this principle, a feminist approach to statutory practice may be more 'controlling' at times than that uninformed by a feminist perspective' (p. 113). They recognize the problem of removing children from their parents and the intrinsic risks involved here.

This brings us to the second difficulty about the power concept and feminism. Instead of seeing power as residing in social roles – i.e. men, *it could equally be considered as a key element in situations*. In feminist analyses, power has been mostly defined perjoratively but the rise of certain individuals to dominant positions may be necessary, in fact, to solve problems; this is often referred to as a task-orientation rather than a social group maintenance approach. The more demanding a situation the more useful powerful individuals can be as long as mechanisms exist to control their excesses. Even within patriarchy power has not been exercised at the same high level as feminists suggest. In the case of children, far fewer are beaten or worked to death or starved than ever before and as we have indicated, the new Children Act advanced their 'autonomy interests' significantly. In other words, times change.

Common experience also shows us that where women are achieving positions of power, for example as politicians, they appear to fight their own corner as aggressively as men. This may not be because they are 'reinforcing the patriarchy principle' but simply because the situation demands it. Further doubts about the feminist optimism for a less aggressive future arise from the general tenor of anti-sexism. As we argued in the previous chapter, radical feminism has been willing to be as aggressive and adversarial as seemed necessary and it is difficult to believe this is something that can be turned up and down, at will, like a volume control.

The greater freedoms for, especially, middle-class, women bring new dilemmas as role conventions change. Madonna is a potent symbol of this, as the following comment implies:

> The point espoused by the designers Gaultier, Galliano and Dolce and Gabbana – who are fashion's new generation – is that using sexual stereotypes in clothing empowers rather than denigrates women. These are clothes as weapons, the conical breasted bra as missile, the corset, armour. Subtle, they're not. When Madonna grabbed her satin-clad Gaultier crotch on stage she wasn't shouting 'Fuck me' but 'Fuck you.' The message is loud and clear. Loud enough to make me long for the whisper of seduction. (*Elle – Guardian*, 9/1/92, p. 15)

At individual family levels the renegotiation of such male–female roles will create strains on both partners and ideological assessments are of only partial value for child-care practitioners.

The future value of feminism

A movement which sets out to fight for fundamental social change will always experience problems of definition, identity and methodology. Feminism is no exception. Its influence is perhaps much wider than it believes and this is nowhere more true than in family and children's matters. In other countries such as Spain where the general pace of change has been much faster in the last fifteen years, the dramatic changes in the position of wives and mothers are even more conspicuous.

For children, the benefits are likely to be that their mothers will be able to protect them better if they have a stronger voice, seriously violent male–female relationships may not be as inescapable as before and we know that women are seeking divorce more often and being awarded sole custody. The growing influence of women may challenge wider economic and employment policies and achieve a fairer distribution of child-care responsibilities.

Earlier comments in this book have described the growth in step-fathers who are having to integrate with existing families, their *association* with sexual abuse and the predominance of men as sexual abusers. Drawing on these findings, heavily influenced by feminist thinking, it might be argued that an increasing child-care role for men could lessen the risk of abuse by enhancing caring qualities.

Despite these potential benefits it will be important for feminism to accept limitations as a causal model of child abuse. The problem of dangerous parents – mothers and fathers – will remain and social workers will be required to protect children from them whatever the wider mitigating circumstances. Poverty, class and racism will also need to be incorporated because of their serious effects on children and families.

Finally the matter of power will present theoretical challenges as more women acquire it. In recent years feminism has had to begin to confront the reality that women commit not only physical, but also sexual abuse (see Allen, 1990; Elliot, 1992, pp. 12–13; Wolfers, 1992, pp. 13–14). If the first task of feminism has been to isolate and extract women from society for analytical purposes, the second stage may be to reinstate them with a stronger identity back into the even more fundamental debate about human relations.

Anti-racism as knowledge

Although anti-racism has had a powerful impact on social work attitudes in general, its influence as a source of knowledge about child abuse has been less significant than that of feminism. First, it is less far-reaching by which is meant that it relates to far fewer individuals in UK society. Cheetham (1986, pp. 12–13) refers to projections for the black population for 1991 of around 2.5 million or 5 per cent of the UK population (whose parents were born in the West Indies, India, Bangladesh, Africa and Pakistan) and about half of them will have been born in this country.

A second reason for arguing that the impact on knowledge has been less is that it is closely linked with class and poverty, factors which have long been acknowledged in social work as contributing to child abuse. To say that amongst the poor, black people are likely to be the poorest redefines existing knowledge rather than creating new. The notion too that certain groups of people are labelled and discriminated against is not a new one.

The importance of anti-racism has been to add an extra dimension to our knowledge of how children can suffer and to create a powerful and distinctive body of detailed information about the history and process of the suffering. In the same way that feminism challenged institutionalized thinking, so anti-racism has revealed many deeply rooted stereotypes used by white people. The writing of Small and Maximé for example (in Ahmed et al., 1986) reveals the psychological pain for black children forced to 'become white' and this therefore adds to our definition knowledge of child abuse. There is the general problem that as black families encounter the welfare services they will be dealt with by more affluent, and thus white, workers and agencies who may have little knowledge of particular ethnic minority cultures. Under-recruitment of black foster parents can lead to similar difficulties but paradoxically a reluctance to place black children with white carers can con-demn them to longer periods in 'temporary' residential care.

In these ways anti-racism has contributed greatly to our definitions of child abuse. As to measuring prevalence the picture is less clear. Earlier statements echoed those of feminism in their universally bleak assessment of the position of black children and families. More recently a more measured approach indicates that prediction is difficult. Research by Gill and Jackson (1983) into trans-racial adoption of black children by white parents sug-gested that the great majority of the children they studied seemed relatively well-adjusted and although this finding has been challenged it remains problematic for anti-racism. The recent Department of Health publication *Patterns and Outcomes in Child Placement* (DoH, 1991e) summarizes current knowledge about black children in care and indicates that the picture is a complex one with wide variations within different age groups in different ethnic groups. In fact it is mixed-race children who appear to be most vulnerable, while Asian children were under-represented in all age groups (pp. 14–17).

A further source of abuse where race is strikingly evident is in juvenile crime. The treatment of black young people by the criminal justice system and the police is well documented (see Brake and Hale, 1992, for a review of the law and order issue). Even if black children have avoided abuse early on they risk police harassment, arrest and custodial sentences dispropor-tionate to their numbers.

As a source of knowledge that leads to specific action anti-racism can con-tribute as does feminism by specifying how the particular as well as the general features of ethnic minority groups relate to abuse. We continue to need more information about how child-rearing is influenced by non-European values, how family structures and parent–child relationships dif-fer, how the use of welfare services is perceived (for black people tend to use services voluntarily less than white people), and how religious beliefs affect their holder's perception of white practices. As with feminism the initial crusading form of knowledge may be reinforced by a more systematic and detailed data base that social workers can use in their work with black families.

A general knowledge for child abuse

After more than twenty years of intense investigation into child abuse there is no prospect of a narrow knowledge base for action. If we return to the analogy with AIDS, it is as if research has continually discovered more and more symptoms until child abuse ends up looking like 'ill-health'.

What began as a specific attempt in the USA in the early 1960s to warn that parents were physically attacking their children has grown into an 'industry of discovery'. Politics and a moral panic have tried to narrow the list of symptoms and causes of abuse to individual carers but for social workers in particular this is ultimately unacceptable for two reasons. First, the practical one that behind every abusing parent lies a tangle of environmental and interactional issues that have to be addressed. Secondly, the more radical traditions in social work, up-dated especially by feminism and anti-racism, make moral as well as intellectual appeals that render a purely individual approach to child abuse unsatisfactory.

The consequences for developing a knowledge base for child abuse are that we may be moving on to a concern with child care in general. It is tempting to say 'moving *back*', but this would be inaccurate. Although the preoccupation with *individual* factors in child abuse has, in my view, been exaggerated we now know much more about what can happen to children at the hands of their carers than we did. A general concern about the development of social work in the early 1970s was that it was losing some of its specialist knowledge and skills in child care. The child abuse alarms that have punctuated the period since have at least restored the focus on children.

Knowledge is partly defined by who is planning to use it. By this, I mean that not all the knowledge available about something is used fully and equally by everyone. Thus there is a limit to how much a child psychotherapist dealing with a very disturbed child 'know' or incorporate in his/her daily work, about socio-economic contributions to the abuse.

Social workers' position, on the other hand, is a much broader one in the sense that the majority are employed by the state and their actions are now more tightly defined by legislation than ever before. Child abuse knowledge for social workers will need to take account of causes, issues of intervention, and consequences not only of the particular abuse but also of their own actions; this is because the social work role has multiple functions: to promote, to investigate, to protect and to act 'in loco parentis'.

An ecological model

Throughout this book various themes have emerged and with them ideas and factors that all relate to child abuse. Because we have defined it widely, more and more things tend to be drawn into the analysis and thus creates obvious problems for practitioners. If child abuse is coming to mean child care in the traditional sense of the word then the field of study becomes enormous. This should not need an apology, however, for most narrow explanations of abuse soon disappoint. The early years of research and theorizing tended to search for the magic answers – psychopathic parents, a parental history of own childhood abuse, individual violence among other things – but this has increasingly given way to a recognition that child abuse is a multi-factorial event and needs an integrated approach (see Browne, 1988, ch. 2, for a summary and a model).

How then to consider the knowledge needed to take an integrated view of abuse that not only incorporates wide and narrow 'pre-disposing' factors but also the 'situational' dynamics at a point in particular individuals' lives into a *risk analysis* (Cooper and Ball, 1987, ch. 4).

We favour a model that draws on *ecological* thinking because of its emphasis on systems where all the components are dynamically linked (see Cooper and Ball, 1987, ch. 7). This is preferable to a more static approach that might say 'poverty causes abuse' or 'some families are dangerous' without adequately addressing the problem for practitioners of assessing and dealing with an interacting series of events.

The ecological model which is used and further developed by Cooper and Ball builds on four systems:

The Microsystem: the close, immediate, day to day sum of experiences, relationships, and settings of an individual.

The Mesosystem: consists of links and relationships between micro systems, the way in which, for a child, experiences and people at home and at school are linked.

The Exosystem: this is in effect someone else's system over which the individual may have no control, but which have an important effect on him. For example the case conference in relation to the abusing parent.

The Macrosystem: the broadest level, the 'broad ideological and political patterns of a particular culture or sub culture'. For example, the sum of society's views about child abuse will ultimately influence all other lower systems. (Whittaker and Garbarino, 1983, pp. 11–15)

These relationships can be expressed diagrammatically to show the relationships between them (Fig. 4.1).

Each circle represents a person in the microsystem. These people will have the most intimate and significant relationships with the child but also, in some cases, with each other as well. Thus there could be a simple parent–child dyad on a larger family system of child, parents and siblings. There might also be someone else outside the family close enough to the child to justify being included in the microsystem.

Beyond the microsystem will be other people, groups or even organizations who have less intimate but still important relationships with the child

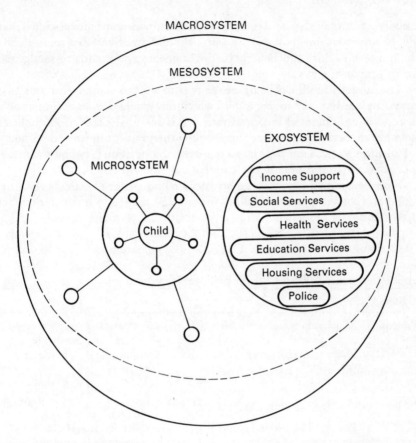

Figure 4.1 Relationships between the four systems of the ecological model

and/or other people in the microsystem. This might be a relative, friend, child-minder, a playgroup, a mothers' support group, an individual teacher or a voluntary organization. The fact that all these 'elements' are important to the child directly or indirectly gives rise to the idea of the mesosystem because the links between them can affect particular relationships and are an important area of work. Thus a child/parent system and a child/school system may not be compatible or again a father may be part of a system with his male friends that influences his attitude towards being a parent. The state services are shown separately because their links with other systems are restricted by their legal position and they may thus influence others more than they are influenced.

The macrosystem is shown as all encompassing. It represents the sum of historical, cultural, political and legal influences that constrain other systems. It may be seen formally as a piece of legislation or as a particular social policy or less explicitly as a cluster of values about family life and childhood. It may also be seen as an attitude, conscious or unconscious, that discriminates against particular groups or individuals within a society. The attitudes and values may belong to a government, a powerful pressure group or to people in general.

The model also allows us to see the way in which state services look two ways, upwards to the macrosystem which ultimately defines them but also across to other parts of the mesosystem; this acknowledges current policies to make the services more interactive with other parts of the mixed economy of welfare. At the same time it is a reminder that welfare is bound by statute and it is only permeable to some extent.

From this model we can begin to allocate knowledge to different systems and parts therein in terms of what needs to be known in order to do what (see Table 4.1).

Table 4.1 Child abuse knowledge from ecosystems

System	Area of knowledge	Purpose
Macro	Social values and attitudes	To understand society's view of children and family life.
	Political ideologies	To understand and estimate social policies.
	Social policy	To understand and estimate the sum and separate impacts on children and families.
	Poverty and discrimination	To identify groups and individuals in need and at risk.
Exo	Agency and Practitioner Values	To understand their relationship to the macrosystem.
	Inter-agency relationships	To promote co-ordinated services and protection policies and practice.
	Agency duties, policies, practice and structures	To develop needs-based assessments. To promote and develop services. To promote partnership with parents. To develop efficient protection and investigation systems. To develop quality substitute care. To develop rehabilitation policies and practice.

Table 4.1 *continued*

System	Area of knowledge	Purpose
	The consequences of Investigation and substitute care (compulsory.)	To diminish 'system abuse'.
Meso	The relationship between state services voluntary and informal networks and resources that centre around the child and family.	To identify and monitor the individual systems and their impact. To promote beneficial systems. To discourage harmful systems. To develop sources of help.
	'Community' development	To encourage partnership, collaboration and empowerment.
Micro	General via the areas listed below	To assess need. To assess risk. To maintain the family *or* to remove the child from the family.
	Individual 'personalities'	To assess individual contributions.
	One to one relationships	To promote beneficial relationships and to 'treat' or sever harmful relationships.
	Family and individual history	To assess the aetiology of the situation.
	Family dynamics	To understand its impact on individuals and relationships.
	External pressures	To distinguish between internal and external factors.
	Damage to child from abuse	To identify consequences and assess degree of likely significant harm.
	Methods of help for victim and other family matters	To provide appropriate counselling or therapy.
	Methods of help for abuser	To estimate whether child's removal from or return to home is possible and appropriate.
	Methods of communication with the child	To understand the child's wishes and feelings.
	Child development	To understand and assess the child's needs.

Integrating the systems

This kind of approach helps to identify the *locations* of knowledge and action to be taken. In incorporates wide political and ideological areas and associated values; the point is also made that at agency levels there may be differing value positions which influence policy and practice. The model also acknowledges that there are positives to be promoted and negatives to be watched carefully and, if necessary, removed. To this extent our approach takes full account of the new Children Act in giving equal weight to promotion and protection. In Chapter 1, I made use of Hardiker et al.'s (1991) ideas about levels and types of intervention by the state. Although their models of developmental, institutional and residual welfare are useful to illustrate trends in the last twenty years of child-care policy, I question their implication that social control is always negative and the result of the failure of service provision. In the same way that the police have a role in protecting the public from dangerous individuals so social work must operate sound and efficient child protection systems for those relatively uncommon situations where voluntary services will not be sufficient or appropriate.

The mesosystem is an important concept because of its recognition of categories of social relationships and connections between them. The question of social isolation and the extent and importance of social support networks appears frequently in child abuse literature. Jones (1991) reviews findings from 'clinical science' (p. 61) about treatment of abusing families. His summary list of factors which make rehabilitation less likely included social isolation (p. 78). Packman et al. (1986) found differences in informal support systems between families whose children came into care and those who did not. Van der Eyken (1982) in assessing *home-start* programmes (intensive volunteer work with families at risk) revealed a dramatic growth in the range and richness of a mother's social networks as her situation improved. Gibbons (1990, ch. 7) found that her survey families referred to social services, when compared with a community sample were less well integrated into the neighbourhood, had moved more often, relied heavily on immediate family members for support and were less satisfied with their neighbourhoods.

Thus the inclusion of the mesosystem as a source of knowledge and help for families is valuable. A sad by-product of the dominance of child protection work is that while social workers have developed extensive and sophisticated relationships with other *official* agencies – and this is the main concern of *Working Together* – they have tended to become more isolated from *informal* networks as their policing role has increased. The demands of agency procedures, the importance of forensic evidence, and the influence of the police in investigations all make it more difficult to develop more fluid and flexible styles of collaboration with unofficial resources. One possible and unwelcome effect of the new Children Act, with its legalistic attention to detail might be to exacerbate this formal style of work.

The ecological model also attempts to be a dynamic rather than static source of knowledge. As family crises develop the actors and events have a reciprocal effect. The family's reaction to the investigation, the social worker's style of intervention and the consequences (maintaining the child at home or removing the child) all alter initial assessments. They have been studied (see Corby, 1987 for examples and the Secretary of State for Social Services (Cleveland Report), 1988) and knowledge is available about them. An ecological approach sees individuals and relationships not merely as passive victims but as actively responding to and influencing events.

For this reason knowledge which focused only on environmental issues would be deficient. Despite the difficulties in identifying individual risk factors in abuse there is a wealth of treatment studies as Jones (1991) indicates that can be drawn on although they need always to be set in socio-economic contexts.

Above all our approach to knowledge for child abuse recognizes the multiple influences on children's situations, those that are at the primary level and are relevant to the whole child population, those at the secondary level which concern targeted services and those at the tertiary level when crises arise. We can also talk of a fourth level of consequences which then influence future abuse either of the child in question or of others. In some ways to distinguish between prevention and 'treatment' is inadequate for today's victim may be tomorrow's abuser and today's abuser perhaps yesterday's victim.

Summary

I have briefly summarized the problems of establishing knowledge in order to explain why child abuse happens, how extensive it is and whether it is predictable and preventable. The impression is that none of these areas offers the kind of certainty that allows a disease model of abuse.

I have given special attention to feminism and anti-racism as sources of knowledge because of their wider importance in re-shaping our views of social inequality. They make useful contributions as value bases and frameworks for action to help families. However, like other explanations they have difficulty at times in separating out other related factors such as poverty and class.

In attempting to set out knowledge requirements I have developed an ecological method description which draws heavily on a systems approach. This brings together the major influences on child abuse, from macro to micro level and relates them in time and space. In the next chapter a theme which runs throughout much current thinking about relationships between the state system and families is considered, namely partnership with parents.

5 / PARENTS

Partnership

Partnership between the state and parents is now on the official child-care agenda. It forms one of the key principles of the Children Act 1989 and is reasserted in the various official documents which accompany it. *Working Together* begins with a section about partnership saying:

> Agencies should ensure that staff who are concerned with the protection of children from abuse understand that this assumption in the Act of *a high degree of co-operation between parents and local authorities* requires a concerted approach to inter-disciplinary and inter-agency working. (DoH, 1991b, para. 1.8; italics added)

Volume 2 of the Act's *Guidance and Regulations* (DoH, 1991c) concerned with Family Support, Day Care and Educational Provision has a section entitled 'Partnership or Compulsion' which indicates that voluntary services are to be considered before children are removed from their families. Volume 3 on Family Placements early on sets out principles of partnership and participation and refers to the need to involve parents and children in decision-making processes, give them explanations of the local authority's powers and duties and actions it may need to take, and consult them before decisions are made about a child 'who is about to be or is already being looked after by a local authority' (para. 2.10). Further parts of the Act and its attendants refer to greater involvements for parents in case reviews and in case conferences as well as written information for parents arising from such situations.

Partnership is given less prominence in Volume 1 of the *Guidance and Regulations* dealing with Court Orders, in contrast to the other volumes. It is most clearly addressed in the section on Child Assessment Orders and their implications for practice (pp. 50–51); this seems logical in that such an order is unlikely to be made if the local authority cannot persuade the court that they *have* tried to collaborate with the parents. Beyond that it is noticeable that, for all the general exhortations about partnership, this particular volume pursues the topic less vigorously than its companions.

All the above material has flowed from the 1989 Act. This is not true of the other important current government document *Protecting Children* which was published in 1988. In terms of partnership, this now looks distinctly dated in its language. Thus, within its section on philosophy and principles, paragraph 4.2 concerned with parents says:

> When child protection agencies intervene in a family, the parents have a right to an open and honest approach from social workers who should provide a clear explanation of their powers, actions and reasons for concern. They should strive to maintain a *constructive* relationship with parents at all times.
>
> Parents should have an opportunity to challenge information held on them and decisions taken that affect them. *They have a right to expect careful assessment of any problems prior to long term decisions being taken.* Their views should be sought and taken into account. (DoH, 1988; italics added)

The purpose of *Protecting Children* is to provide guidelines for an assessment of the child(ren) and the family after the initial investigation (of abuse) is completed. I referred previously to McBeath and Webb's (1990–1) criticism of the document's heavily individual approach. It is essentially concerned with how the child and the family are functioning and is noticeably less detailed about environment issues; short sections on Networks, Finance and Physical Conditions (i.e housing) come near the end. Perhaps more significantly there is a section on 'The Concept of Dangerousness' drawing on the work of Dale et al. (1986). This approach has been explored and challenged (Parton and Parton, 1989, pp. 60–73) because of its focus on family dynamics and prediction rather than on media issues.

The concept of dangerousness is also extended to social workers. They may increase the risk of a child being abused or further abused if they are over-optimistic about the family, become over-involved, or fail to detect dangerous patterns of behaviour – in other words if they *under-react*. However Cooper and Ball (1987, ch. 4) argue that social workers can also become 'hazardous' if they *over-react* by taking action precipitately and exclude parents from the investigation process. *Protecting Children* barely acknowledges this issue although *Working Together* makes references (see ch. 2) to the need for sensitive interviewing.

These different emphases are very important to current child abuse work for, as we have indicated previously, social workers' actions are now more closely prescribed than ever before. How, then, does this affect the partner-ship issue? If, or perhaps when, *Protecting Children* is up-dated will it acknowledge a greater role for parents in assessments or will the principle continue to look less firm the more it confronts the realities of abuse allega-tions? Is partnership a realistic and practical proposition or is it a well-intentioned but essentially political statement? Is it, even, a prudent attempt by the Government to distance itself from the embarrassment of another Cleveland? What is clear is that social workers regularly confront situations where partnership is far from easy.

Compulsion

The best test of partnership with families comes in these circumstances where it seems to be failing. If we examine patterns in social workers' relationships with children's families it appears that the picture has become more bleak in the last eighteen years since the Maria Colwell inquiry. Various writers discussed in earlier chapters have identified a move away from voluntary to compulsory work (Packman, 1981; Parton, 1985 and 1991; Cooper and Ball, 1987; Holman, 1988). The use of Place of Safety Orders (POSOs) replaced by Emergency Protection Orders in the Children Act 1989, is a useful indicator of the use in such work and the way it has responded dramatically to child abuse inquiries. Before the Maria Colwell inquiry there were in England 204 POSOs in 1972 (31 March) but afterwards in 1976, 759. Using through the year figures there were 5471 in 1978 rising to 7780 in 1988 after the Jasmine Beckford and Cleveland inquiries (Parton, 1991, pp. 35 and 54).

The number of children on child protection registers gives a further indica-tion of the growth of child-care work. It would be wrong to label all these situations as compulsory for they include referrals by children themselves, parents' relatives and others and thus could be seen as requests for service; on the other hand, there is always an element, if not of compulsion, then at least of conflict when child protection investigations are initiated.

NSPCC register figures referred to earlier covered around 10 per cent of the child population. The number of children registered through 1977 for all kinds of abuse was 997 (Birchall, 1989, p. 17). By 1988, figures for the whole population show 13,300 registrations for the year (DoH, 1988, p. 21). Figures for sexual abuse show a much more dramatic rise being *seven* for 1977 in the NSPCC figures (giving a national projection of 70) but 3900 in 1988 national figures. Creighton (1988, p. 37) also confirms this steep rise, saying of NSPCC registrations: 'In 1981 3 per cent of the abused children had been sexually assaulted. By 1986 this had risen to 31.5 per cent.'

Another feature of the register figures is that they include unsubstantiated suspicion. In the comparison figures given above the category of 'grave con-cern' has been omitted. However, it is a very common reason for registering

a child, accounting for a further 7600 (36 per cent) on top of the 1988 figure
of 13,300. It is important to remember that child protection registers
measure official concern rather than proven incidence of child abuse. The
figures represent judgements by child protection workers normally arrived
at through case conferences which are not the same as court hearings.

'False positives'

It is inevitable, statistically, that as the child protection net has been cast ever
wider it is likely to catch the wrong fish. It is beyond the scope of this book
to review the problem of accurate measurement and prediction (but see
Kotelchuck, 1982, ch. 3 and Dingwall, 1989, ch. 2). Although much of the
research has been concerned with broad screening of 'at risk' families it is
very relevant to child protection registrations for the latter are themselves
making predictions about families who are causing concern. Kotelchuck
points out that in a hypothetical population of 1000 children, even if it is
assumed that child abuse is happening to 10 per cent of them 'it would be
predicted that 225 children would be likely to be child abuse and neglect
cases when they would, in fact, *not* be child abuse and neglect cases' (p. 101).
It is this group who are termed false positives.

As well as the statistical problems there is also an underlying moral issue.
If we are to protect children what level of error is society willing to accept
which might wrongly draw innocent families into the net? This is of the same
order of moral and strategic dilemma that faced the American military in
Vietnam. Their saturation bombing and chemical defoliation had
undesirable side-effects but was justified because it also killed or disrupted
the Viet Cong.

The moral problem is clearly more acute than if child protection is
approached from a more positive point of view. Apart from the obvious
financial difficulties no-one is likely to object to a policy of providing good
preventive welfare services to *all* young families. Not only does such a policy
have benefits for everyone, it may make a significant difference to the very
small percentage of families who are likely to become abusing. Unfortunately, because of the general decline in universal preventive services we
are brought back to the more negative dilemmas of which families to label
as 'dangerous'.

Underwager (1987) in his evidence to the Cleveland Inquiry provides
figures to show that in the USA the problem of false positives is a real one.
Besharov, an ex-director of the US National Centre on Child Abuse and
Neglect suggested in 1987 that

> about 65 per cent of all reports of child abuse are labelled unfounded
> after investigation. This is in sharp contrast to 1975 when only about
> 35 per cent of all reports were unfounded. (Quoted by Amphlett, 1988,
> p. 7)

In the heightened atmosphere of relationship breakdown and child custody disputes the problem can become even worse: 'There is no faster way to get sole custody than to accuse a spouse of sexually abusing his child' (Wakefield and Underwager, 1988, p. 329).

Effects on families

Current child protection work has certain features. It is tightly regulated by law and procedures. Police are major partners along with social workers. The fear of making a mistake, of seeing a child subsequently abused or killed, is very strong in the light of numerous child abuse inquiries. These features clearly create great pressures not only on workers in the field but also on the families themselves. In this climate partnership may be the first victim. The following case example taken from the Open University's training pack *The Children Act 1989: Putting it into Practice* (1991) reveals some of the dilemmas facing practitioners wishing to work in partnership with parents.

Edward's story

Edward Grey is nine, and an only child. His father, Colin, is a freelance consultant engineer; his mother, Eleanor, is an accountant. For the last six months Colin Grey has been living and working in a town some 200 miles away, returning to be with his family at weekends.

This Monday, Edward came to school looking very upset and as though he had not slept at all. Miss Taylor, his form teacher, who knows Edward well, spoke to him at break time and he started to tell her that something was wrong. She had already noticed that Edward was showing signs of distress and anxiety, and wondered whether it was to do with his dad going away, or because of rows between his parents. She had heard that the marriage was going through a rough patch.

After a few false starts, Edward had told her that somebody – though he refused adamantly to say who – has been '. . . doing rude things he didn't like' to him. This person, Edward said, threatened him that terrible things would happen if he told anybody. Edward was clearly very upset and extremely frightened. However, after some more talk he grudgingly agreed that Miss Taylor would need to talk to another teacher, and that his mum would have to know too.

The upshot of the investigation that followed is an impasse. The procedure agreed by the social services department was followed and from what Edward told the social worker and police officer who interviewed him it was decided that a medical examination would be necessary to establish whether medical indications of sexual abuse could be found. The social services are anxious that a medical examination should be carried out straightaway to see if Edward is injured or infected and before any forensic evidence is lost. Mrs Grey is concerned about this. She says she is willing for an examination to be carried out, but not until she has had a chance to talk to her husband. She has tried to contact him and so far has not been able to track him down because he is not where she had been told he would be. Things between them, she says, are very strained, and for her to act without his agreement would be the final straw. She dare not say yes to such a major step without discussing it with him. She also wants to take legal advice.

There are no serious concerns about allowing Edward to go home with his mother and the investigative team are working closely with Mrs Grey, and want to progress as sensitively as possible. But at the same time, what may be critical medical evidence could be lost unless Edward is examined very soon.

What is known in this case? The account does not make clear exactly what Edward said and how much detail he has provided about what he says was done to him. However, the view of the social services is that a medical examination is necessary 'very soon'. This may seem straightforward but in fact there are two elements to this desire for an examination: first, to see if Edward is 'injured or infected' and, secondly, so that 'critical medical evidence' is not lost. Now these are not the same thing and it may be that they have different implications. As we understand it, evidence of penetration through traces of semen may disappear within forty-eight hours, in which case if abuse occurred over the weekend then, from the forensic point of view, every hour is precious. If a medical examination aims to protect Edward's health it may not be quite so urgent because there is nothing in the account to suggest that he is apparently injured or that his life is in danger. Thus it is the *forensic* issue which is the most urgent and it has to be established that the gathering of such evidence is also in Edward's *overall* best interests.

Edward's mother is not objecting to an examination but she does want to contact her husband first; unfortunately she cannot immediately track him down. Until she does she is, in effect, refusing to co-operate. In legal terms the social services could argue, first, that they have reason to believe that Edward is suffering or is likely to suffer significant harm, and secondly, that because 'access' to him is being frustrated, in the special circumstances of this case, this constitutes an emergency. It is assumed that the lack of time would preclude a full hearing of an application for a Child Assessment Order which would, of course, secure an examination of Edward. Therefore they could seek an Emergency Protection Order (Children Act 1989, Section 44(1)(b)). The court *must* consider whether Edward is likely to suffer significant harm *in the future* if they do not make the order and presumably social services would argue that the loss of medical evidence would make it more difficult to establish the abuser's identity, if indeed there is one:

if they (or rather the police) fail to do this Edward could be abused again.

Even if the court was persuaded by the social services argument and granted the emergency order the matter is still not simple. The order does not lead *automatically* to the child's removal from home; how and when this should happen and how long it should last remains at the court's discretion. In this case the account says that, 'There are no serious concerns about allowing Edward to go home with his mother.' The appropriate course for the court therefore might be to grant the order and stipulate that Edward should remain away from home *only long enough* for a medical examination to be carried out.

This course seems appropriate and feasible legally and it would seem to reduce family disruption to a minimum. Whether it would be followed in practice is less certain. The author has recently set this case as a problem solving exercise to two groups of final-year social work students. Most of them opted for the course described above but their accounts tended not to distinguish between the two reasons for seeking a medical examination. More seriously they did not often refer to the legal requirement that the child's removal from home should only last as long as safety considerations dictate; those who missed this seemed to assume that the emergency order means removal from home unconditionally.

The point is taken that what students write in college does not equate with what qualified social workers, supported by senior staff and lawyers, might do in practice. It is nevertheless concerning that the students in question make such assumptions; they also had the real advantage of being able to reflect on the problem at leisure, unaffected by the real-life pressures faced by busy practicing social workers. The students, almost without exception, also seemed to dismiss Edward's father from their immediate calculations.

This section is entitled partnership and Edward's case asks important questions. How might a social worker seek Mr Grey's wishes and feelings as required in Section 22(4)(b) of the 1989 Act? Remarkably, hardly any of the students applied their minds to this, simply accepting that Mr Grey was unavailable, and a number assumed automatically that *he* was the abuser. In feedback it was suggested to the students that the considerable resources of the social services and the police might well be able to track down Mr Grey. If that were achieved and if he endorsed his wife's consent for a medical examination then it seems clear that an emergency order would not be necessary. If, of course, he refused then the situation would be different. It might be that his refusal would arouse his wife's suspicions and she would then consent on her own volition; this would be quite legal and the examination could then proceed unless, of course, Edward refused.

Edward's case is skilfully devised to highlight legal and practice dilemmas for child protection workers. But beyond, or perhaps before the law lie the value, assumptions and priorities of workers. How valid is the concept of partnership particularly when the 1989 Act suggests that it should be done where 'practicable' (Section 22(4))? How far are workers prepared to go to avoid the last resort of court action? Does partnership lose its attraction against understandable temptation to 'play safe?' We acknowledge the enormous pressures on child protection workers who may be the focus of anxieties felt by police, senior colleagues, other agencies and, ever in the background, the media and society. Even so the 1989 Act which has been largely welcomed by child protection agencies is insistent on the importance of partnership – it is not an optional extra.

Parents Against INjustice (PAIN)

'Innocents at risk'

PAIN was set up in 1985 by Sue Amphlett and her husband, after being investigated by social services about one of their children who was subsequently shown to be suffering from brittle bone disease. The Amphletts were so shocked and distressed at being victims of child protection investigation that they decided to set up a movement whose aim was to offer help to other families who had suffered similar experiences. An early publication emphasized their concern for 'innocent' parents (1986).

For the first 18 months or so the group existed on small donations and grants until it was awarded a Department of Health grant of £10,000 in 1987, rising to £24,000 for 1989. In 1990 PAIN was awarded a three-year grant of £35,000 per annum. It has always been a small group often consisting of Sue Amphlett as full-time director supported by a secretary and a part-time clerk. Total income has been small – £52,528 in 1989 and £56,114 in 1990. Despite this and despite regular financial difficulties PAIN has been prolific in its activities, producing articles, booklets, guidance, press releases, letters to the Minister of Health, a lengthly submission to the Cleveland Inquiry as well as proposals for twenty-five amendments to the Children Act 1989. Sue Amphlett with the help of voluntary trustees has also appeared regularly on radio and television and contributed various articles to newspapers and journals in the public domain.

As PAIN became established and better known its advice work for parents grew quickly. The 1989–90 Annual Report refers to thirty new cases each week, compared with fifteen to twenty the previous year. Advice was already being offered to 700 families and the group had built up 1300 written case histories. To cope with demand for advice eleven regions were established in the UK served by voluntary regional advisers backed by an administrative system of case forms, procedural guidelines, a steady flow of articles about child abuse and training seminars.

By December 1989 the organization was running into difficulties because of the turnover of regional advisers and a shortage of funds. As a result no new cases could be taken on; this crisis was eventually resolved, but more recently PAIN has had to review its activities because of the continual problem of demand exceeding supply. Like many small voluntary organizations it teetered between the devil and the deep blue sea. Publicity was essential both to promote PAIN's message and to attract funds, but that same publicity also brought fresh requests for help.

The 1990–1 Annual Report recorded that PAIN had submitted proposals for amendments to the Children Bill, set up lists of specialist doctors for second opinions on children, advised solicitors, maintained its promotional and public education activities, received 280 calls from the media during February and March 1991 and continued in its attempts to advise individual families. In June 1990 a National Adviser/Counsellor was appointed to provide a more consistent and co-ordinated service. This was necessary because funds remained inadequate and regions had difficulty retaining advisers.

PAIN took action in particular areas. Their contacts with families revealed a growing tendency of social services departments to persuade alleged abusers to leave their families, and this was termed 'voluntary ousting'. A typical situation was that a family would be warned that an emergency order application was being made to remove the child unless the suspected abuser was 'willing' to leave the family home. In one case recorded by PAIN

> The mother came to us fourteen months after the father had been ousted. At this stage the family was seriously in debt and the marriage was on the point of breaking up. Furthermore the father had only been allowed to see his children twice in the last six months in a social services department and for a period of an hour at a time. There was no verbal or written agreement with the social workers regarding the investigation and they were refusing to allow the father back into the home. The family had spoken to a solicitor who had told them there was nothing they could do as no legal action had been taken. The mother was so frightened of being thought by social workers to be unco-operative because she had asked for outside help that she refused to give her address or telephone number. After this initial contact we heard no more. (PAIN, 1990, p. 6)

The 'ousting' report which also included cases of compulsory ousting ordered by courts was sent to the Minister of Health. PAIN's concerns were twofold: first, they pointed out that measures designed to protect children could also succeed in threatening the family's finances and their housing causing additional stress. Secondly, because the parent was persuaded to move out early in the investigation before any formal legal action was taken either by police or social services, the ousted parent was in an impossible situation legally, having neither a proper forum to protest his or her innocence nor the right to legal aid. The suspected parents frequently found themselves excluded, unable to see their children or even sometimes, to discuss the situation fully with social workers. A decision by the police not to initiate a criminal prosecution would not necessarily alleviate matters because child protection is based on civil law.

Response to Rochdale and Orkney

We have referred previously to the above events which received wide publicity. In both cases PAIN interviewed all the families involved – six, with twenty children in Rochdale and four with nine children in Orkney and summarized 'Headline Points' of concern. For Rochdale these were:

1 Children have been denied access to their families for several months.
2 The families have neither been informed about nor involved in the case conference and registration process.
3 There have been no home and social assessments.
4 Parents have not been informed by Social Services of their own legal rights and statutory powers, duties and roles of the agencies involved.
5 The parents' views have not been sought on any matters.
6 Parents have not been informed about complaints procedures.
7 Children have, once again, been removed from their beds.
8 Rochdale Social Services have failed to observe their own guidelines.
9 Rochdale Social Services have failed to implement minimum good working practice as required by the Department of Health guidelines *Working Together*.

(PAIN, 1990, p. 2)

Less than a year later the same concerns were listed in a further report (PAIN, March 1991, pp. 1–2) on the Orkney situation. In both reports examples are given to support the complaints made by parents of the families involved. If these complaints are to be believed they give an impression of child protection procedures driven by forensic considerations with some children virtual prisoners within the rescue system, shut off not only from their parents but also relatives, friends and personal possessions.

Both in Rochdale and Orkney, and more generally in other cases known to PAIN, the exclusion of parents from case conferences was frequently commented on. The Cleveland Inquiry was quite clear in its recommendation that this should be the rare exception rather than the rule but some Area Child Protection Committees who formulate local protection policies had made little progress in this matter several years later.

Parton (1991, p. 197) considered that PAIN's 'direct influence and lobbying upon the Children Bill was marginal' although it was 'important in helping to frame some of the central issues at play during the Cleveland affair.' Certainly parliamentary debates on the Children Bill mainly took place during the spring and summer of 1989 and drew heavily on themes existing before PAIN became most active. Even so we can see points at which the eventual Act does acknowledge some of the issues raised by the group. Parental attendance at case conferences is now accepted, parents who volunteer to leave the family home can be offered help (including money) by social services departments, contact between children in compulsory care and their parents is expected to be the rule unless there are special reasons otherwise and the new Child Assessment Order supported by PAIN now offers a less drastic procedure for carrying out medical assessments where abuse is suspected. Despite this, social services practice in some areas still falls short of new requirements.

The Orkney Inquiry is still in progress so its findings remain unknown. Because of its particular geography the question arises of partnership not just with parents but also with the whole island community. A crucial issue is the fact that all the children were removed to substitute care on the mainland; this has interesting implications for the way child protection services use (or don't use) local resources and networks which, in the late 1970s and early 1980s were major goals for social work. If protective social work is unable to work in partnership it will come to resemble the police more and more. For many families this means an unwelcome knock on the door and the full weight and rigour of the law.

Current PAIN work

Present pressures on PAIN have limited its initial advice work which has proved very time-consuming. A current proposal is to offer a befriending service that would serve to put families involved in the investigation system with others who have had similar experiences. This has, however, created new difficulties; families under suspicion may aggravate their situation if it becomes known to social services and police that they are associating with other suspected abusers! It should also be remembered that as an organization PAIN has never made judgements as to whether individuals have or have not committed abuse. To some extent this has proved irrelevant in the light of parents' complaints. As the Children Act and its guidelines make clear, partnership is not dependent on innocence or guilt. In addition PAIN see their role as providing advice which will help to clarify whether or not abuse has taken place.

PAIN is perhaps moving into a second consolidatory and more specialized phase. Records are now being kept of fathers separated from their children following allegations of sexual abuse by their ex-partners and this will generate a report in due course. A further area of interest is the position of non-familial carers accused of abusing children, be they child-minders, baby-sitters, foster parents or residential staff; such people have also turned to PAIN for help bringing particular problems and needs. The wealth of case material possessed by the Group is an obvious research source and a current project undertaken by an independent team is collating and analysing the experiences and views of children and their families caught up in investigations. The Children Act itself is clearly of importance and there is a present exercise to monitor how children in compulsory care are having contact with parents, grandparents and other family members.

One of PAIN's most important findings is that when families are mistakenly accused of child abuse they can undergo traumata which are both extreme and unusual. Because of this experience the group is currently looking to employ a counsellor with skills drawn from disaster crisis work where a form of psychological de-briefing is the most important element.

PAIN has always been sensitive to and sensible of accusation that it may, at times, be guilty of defending the indefensible if parents who contact the group have in fact abused their children. It is for this reason that much of the work has aimed at constructive proposals for law and procedure. The group has offered advice, consultancy and training for child protection workers and sees this as an important area for future development. The research mentioned earlier will also be important in quantifying better PAIN's work to date.

Although PAIN has pursued a very distinctive line it has also, at times, made common cause with other influential pressure groups. The Family Rights Group had similar concerns and submitted evidence to the Cleveland Inquiry; like PAIN they identified investigation interviews with parents and children, information to parents, case conferences and contact as issues needing urgent attention. The Children's Legal Centre and the Children's Society also contributed evidence.

Child protection side-effects

What emerges from the work of PAIN and other children and family groups is that the child protection system and process in its present form carries its own risks. The growth of concern and reports about sexual abuse has particularly highlighted these risks because it deals with areas which are inevitably grey, where secrecy may operate and where, in the absence of hard evidence, protection workers may rely heavily on getting 'confessions'. Yet, paradoxically, it is in such areas that social services power under civil law may be most sharply defined because the *threat* of removing children is so devastating to families.

In such situations partnership is easily undermined. This applies to parents who have abused as well as to those who have not for the legalistic nature of child protection can actually inhibit dialogue. Social workers may often say that they cannot begin to 'work with' abusers until they admit the offence. However, it is obvious that any admission of guilt carries frightening consequences – criminal prosecution and likely imprisonment with the added burden of hostility and even violence from other prisoners who hold 'nonces', as they are called, in special contempt. The UK approach to child abuse is liable to process individuals direct from confession into the criminal system without any intervening possibilities of help or therapy.

The Netherlands has, for some time operated a 'confidential doctor' system that does provide this missing link (Van Montfoort, 1990). If abusers admit their offence they are offered treatment by a multi-disciplinary team which has legal discretion whether to notify the police. Only if the prospects for safe rehabilitation of the family and the offender look unlikely will they bring in criminal procedures. Although the Dutch approach is not without its problems, especially in the areas of natural justice, it deserves study. The UK alternative seems to offer to the abuser little but a very bleak future and this may have unwanted consequences for the family. O'Hagan (1989, pp. 72–3) indicates these problems by pointing to situations where, once sexual abuse has been uncovered, the abusers have committed suicide and in some cases killed their children and/or their partners. For this reason work by Wyre (1989, ch. 33) to offer treatment to abusers as an alternative to prison merits much attention.

Principles of partnership

The Family Rights Group provide a clear and concise rationale for partnership (1991) that effectively combines fundamental values, pragmatism and lessons from research. PAIN in their turn have produced a new booklet *Working in Partnership* (Amphlett, 1991) designed to help families faced with investigations but which contains much of interest for child protection workers.

I suggest that the essence of partnership for workers can be expressed as the five Is:

Integrity
Information
Involvement
Interest
Interpretation

Integrity requires workers to have an honest appreciation of their powerful position in child protection and to convey their legal functions clearly to families whom they are investigating. Workers may have an understandable reluctance to be seen as interrogators and may try to portray themselves as 'wanting to offer help'. It is essential that this approach takes account of families' anxieties. Hence parental reluctance to co-operate in investigations may not always indicate guilt but, as PAIN often found, may instead reflect a genuine distrust of social workers.

The Children Act re-affirms and clarifies child protection functions. Natural justice as well as practical considerations require that workers are open and precise in explaining their purposes and this may involve taking trouble to define exactly what the functions are and how, for example, they differ from the role of the police and how civil law differs from criminal law.

Information or rather the lack of it has often been a complaint of families under investigation. The complexities of the child protection system, the roles of various workers and agencies and the possible outcomes are not likely to be well understood. Similarly parents must be told about their own rights, about their legal position, about access to official files and about complaints procedures.

As investigations proceed and particularly if children are removed from home, parents may feel isolated and left in the dark. They will require to be kept up-to-date, receive written information about conferences, reviews and decisions, even where they have attended, and generally to understand what is happening. The Children Act makes an important contribution here by providing for judicial Directions Hearings at which parents' solicitors can discover and discuss local authorities' evidence and intentions.

Involvement lies at the heart of partnership. Understandably workers may wish and need to exclude parents at times in order to ensure children's safety. However, the great majority of children under investigation continue to live with their parents (Family Rights Group, 1991, p. 15) so their families are continuing and central features of their lives. Even where children have to enter care families remain very important and will be the place to which most of them return (Millham et al., 1986).

Involvement should also be extended to other people, to grandparents, relatives and family friends who may well have important contributions to make (Family Rights Group, 1991, pp. 8–9). PAIN recorded on their paper on the Orkney situation that relatives and friends who offered to accommodate the children in question appeared to receive little attention from social services (PAIN, 1991, p. 5).

Interest is closely related to involvement. The Beckford Inquiry Report was critical of social workers for allegedly forgetting that their client was the child not the family. The Children Act redresses this simplistic view but the pressure on workers to keep the child's welfare paramount may lead them to relegate the needs of the parents. For our purposes here, it is a question of how workers communicate. Do the parents feel marginalized or devalued, as incidentals in the process? Abusers are human too. Some of the extreme hostility towards people who sexually abuse their children comes from within social work itself, perhaps traceable to feminist concerns to expose and challenge male power. Unfortunately, the rejected abuser does not disappear forever but may re-emerge into the same or other families in the future.

Social work is never easy. Child protection sets an enormous challenge to promote the welfare of children while at the same time retaining a genuine and active compassion for all of those who are connected to them.

Interpretation refers to the fact that there are no simple truths in child care. Parents sometimes get the impression that the child protection system operates on the basis of systematic and secure knowledge and that procedures are cast in stone. In truth, this work depends heavily on assessing risk and taking risks (Cooper and Ball, 1987, ch. 4) and this means making professional judgements.

The Children Act is much more prescriptive than its predecessors but as we saw in Edward's case interpretation of events, motives and possible outcomes is a very uncertain business. Again this brings us back to dialogue between workers and families, to sharing of concerns and opinions and to negotiation. In legal terms, the next few years are likely to produce no shortage of case law about how key sections of the new legislation should be interpreted; this applies equally to professional judgements.

Overall, then, partnership remains a key element in child abuse work. The events of the last twenty years have greatly undermined the image of child protection workers as offering a service to and in agreement with families. Instead they are likely to be seen as official intruders, remote and suspicious. The events in Cleveland, Rochdale and Orkney illustrate the extreme end of this process and perhaps the Children Act is an official recognition that a balance needs to be restored. Faced with a chronic shortage of resources social workers have good reason to find this a daunting task; but research evidence confirms the importance of families for children and there is beyond that the important humane principle that co-operation enriches everyone more than compulsion.

Summary

We have identified the importance of partnership between child protection workers and families as a key issue legally, practically and morally. Partnership has become increasingly threatened by the growth in compulsion and conflict as central features of child-care work in the last twenty years.

The development, experiences and influence of PAIN have been explored at length as a symbol of failures in partnership. The findings of this and other family promotion groups have helped to redefine the essence of partnership. I have proposed that this essence can be expressed by the five Is – Integrity, Information, Involvement, Interest and Interpretation – and suggested how these can be addressed in practice. Just as the last decade or so has produced much material about the dangers, the extent and the causes of child abuse, so, now, workers can draw on evidence that partnership is not only vital but also achievable. The discussions of partnership in this chapter have focused particularly on parents. We now need to look at children themselves in child abuse, both as victims and as contributors to their own welfare.

6 / CHILDREN

Expectations of social workers

Worker demand and supply

Current UK social work courses last two years. During this short period students are required to develop a sound set of values, learn the statutory duties and provisions of local authorities not just towards children but to all client groups, acquire a social science base that includes an appreciation of multi-cultural, economic and political aspects, explore assessment and methods of intervention, practice social work skills and divide their time between college and agency placements.

Returning to children, CCETSW expects all students at the point of qualification to know something about children and their families and:

> Essential for the qualified worker will be the ability to create effective means of communication for all the members of the family concerned. This includes communication with the child or young person within their own family as well as when accommodated elsewhere. (CCETSW, 1991a, p. 18)

This communication will depend heavily on knowing what and who children are, how they develop, what their needs are and how they are affected when things go wrong. This is a tall order for any student on any course but particularly so for social workers. The enormous increase in concern about child abuse in the last twenty years has led to corresponding pressure on a training system which still aims to train workers generically, that is to be able to transfer knowledge, skill and practice across numerous settings and client groups. As we have seen, too, child-care law has become more complex and protection procedures more legalistic.

This begs the question why the growth in child-care concern has not led to an irresistible demand for specialist training and qualifications in child-care, if not in basic training then later at post-qualifying level. A model already exists in the mental health field where the more complex work involving the removal of client's liberties can *only* be done by social workers who have passed an advanced examination and become Approved Social Workers (ASWs). In child care we are far from this point. CCETSW's firm requirements about basic training 'competencies' are not matched by their expectations of employers after qualification either to provide protection for workers from the most difficult work regarding child abuse or appropriate in-service and secondment to post-qualifying courses.

Some students will have specialized in child care as 'an area of particular practice' but this will obviously not include *responsibility* for child protection work. Other students will not have had this special experience but it is quite possible and legal for hard-pressed local authorities to employ these people to do the same kind of work. CCETSW again: 'Newly qualified workers *cannot* be expected to take prime responsibility for this kind of work' (italics added) and:

> Not all social workers are able to undertake child protection work; some are unable to resolve the value conflicts in this work. Even so all workers have an individual and collective responsibility to ensure that collusion with bad practice or management is avoided. This should be part of discussions in the first year after qualification. (CCETSW, 1991a, pp. 94–5)

The whole tone of this crucial part of CCETSW's latest guidance on child abuse work is noticeably hesitant. Newly qualified staff should be protected and should be given additional training and an apprentice type experience. This is not, however, expressed as a commandment but rather as a pious hope, especially through the use of 'cannot' in the earlier quotation rather than 'must not'. In many local authorities the reality is that new staff *are* well supported and modern child protection guidelines strongly discourage independent individual action anyway. But equally, well-staffed departments in temporary difficulties or badly staffed ones generally, are not always inhibited from misusing staff in the belief that any service is better than none at all. The Cleveland Inquiry drew attention to the pressures of child protection work and Brian Roycroft, then President of the Association of Directors of Social Services, in commenting on Cleveland Social Services Departments' earlier worthy attempts to improve their practice, said:

> But, like most Departments, when faced with a flood of requests for investigation, they would of necessity have to deploy staff who were less knowledgeable and skilled. (Secretary of State for Social Services, 1988, p. 85)

and David Jones, General Secretary of BASW commented:

I find it incredible that the public are expecting social workers to handle these difficult cases, are ready to hand down sweeping criticisms of the way they are handled, but yet we are not provided with the resources for even updating training, and the training commitment from the Personal Social Services to a post-qualifying (PQ) level has been poor. (Ibid., p. 217)

Although the events of Beckford and Cleveland had an effect particularly on in-service training, the situation remains 'poor' and aggravated by the current economic recession. As to why we do not have a child-care equivalent of the ASW we can only speculate. What is clear is that the extent and cost of child protection is much greater than for mental health work and this must be a major factor. CCETSW has recently published useful discussions and recommendations which will offer a firm base for action but the extent of the challenge is considerable as they indicate thus:

the total annual budget available for approved PQ training for *all* social workers (45,000) in the UK (£301,700 in 1986/7 and £436,000 in 1989/90) is roughly equivalent to the available annual budget for 240 GP trainees in *only two* regional health authorities (approximately £360,000). (CCETSW, 1991b, p. 185)

In Chapter 1, we questioned the then Government's real commitment to improving local authority child protection work. The consequences are evident in the present sad situation where the state is still unwilling to offer adequate minimum guarantees to children in need about the level of help they can expect from social workers. If our society is to go beyond rhetoric in its concern for children it must accept that care costs money and that social workers are a vital resource.

Functions, tasks and the need to know

Given the great demands on social workers in the child-care field it is essential to look realistically but effectively at what they need to know. In the previous chapter we focused on work in partnership with parents; here the emphasis is on knowledge about children and on local authority social workers. Although important social work with and for children takes place outside the local authority setting it is only here that a unique cluster of roles and tasks emerges which demands a special range of knowledge about children. As Table 6.1 shows, those tasks are extensive but a distinctive feature is the way they are *shared* at different points with workers from other disciplines who all contribute expertise.

What makes local authority social workers unique is the way they are involved throughout the child-care process once a referral has been received. It therefore follows that they need *some* knowledge of the way children

Table 6.1 The child-care process

	Those involved at various stages		With special knowledge of
Referral ↓	The public	→	Views of childhood.
	The local community	→	Local norms and children's needs.
	Local networks	→	Contact with and support to children.
Investigation ↓	The police	→	Criminal law investigation techniques.
	Schoolteachers	→	Children's social and educational development goals and norms.
Assessment ↓	Medical staff (GPs, Health Visitors, Nurses, Paediatricians, Child Psychiatrists)	→	Children's development, health, illness and disturbance.
	Lawyers	→	The children's court system.
Decisions ↓	Psychologists	→	Children's behaviour.
	Therapists	→	Children's counselling and therapy.
Consequences (Services or into care.)	Care Staff (Day-care, Foster Parents, Residential Staff)	→	Working and living with children.
	The family	→	The child's history and temperament.
	AND		
	The child	→	His/her own needs, wishes, feelings, hopes and fears.

feature as actors and victims at all the different phases in the process and this indicates the eclectic difficulties for social workers. Except for the family and the child, other participants in the process have roles which are restricted in place and also in time in most cases; they have less need to understand the way the child will move through and be affected by the process. This was dramatically illustrated in Cleveland where paediatricians did not limit themselves to making diagnoses but also strongly recommended court orders to remove the children from home without apparent appreciation of the problems this created in the care system. (Secretary of State for Social Services, 1988, p. 84). At other times lawyers may argue persuasively for the return of children to their parents because the child expresses a wish, without fully understanding the significance or dangers of such a wish. Police may wish to pursue a child abuse investigation in order to secure a conviction and not appreciate the stress that this will cause to the child if it is not handled with sensitivity.

Despite these difficulties other workers bring expertise to their parts of the process. The same skills which make the police threatening to children also contain lessons in how to have focused communication with them. Lawyers in court need to tune their questioning very precisely to the child's intelligence, understanding and anxiety. Schoolteachers will have a fund of experience about 'normal' child behaviour in a social setting; they will have the benefit, often, of a longitudinal view of behaviour and school performance which makes it easier to spot sudden or gradual deteriorations: the increasing listlessness and shabbiness of the neglected child, the timidity or bullying of the battered child, the precocious sexuality of the sexually abused child or the indiscriminate over-friendliness of the emotionally deprived child; and they will also have the barometer of attendance registers. Playgroup or nursery school workers will bring similar expertise with the extra benefit of working more closely with smaller groups of children.

Other staff, be they GPs, health visitors or paediatricians, will have expert knowledge of developmental norms, sources of delay or damage and medical consequences of abuse. Consequences will also be the special province of therapists who may work with young and older children suffering both initial and long term effects of abuse. Psychologists can often contribute formal methods of assessing children's behaviour as well as programmes of treatment alongside child psychiatrists and therapists. Care staff's contributions will be a mixture of training and experience about direct interaction with children, their strengths and vulnerabilities and the meaning for them of potent symbols such as carers, accommodation and times of the day and night; all these may be crucial pieces of information both in the assessment and in the later helping phases of the process.

This account does not neglect the non-professional contributions. Friends, neighbours and local networks will be aware not only of the child in question but also of the child's everyday social context. Their great importance is that they are around when the professionals are not, in the early mornings, evenings, night-times and at weekends. In the case of seven year-old Maria Colwell it was the local shopkeeper who was one of the first to express concern because she was sent to his shop to collect and carry home heavy bags of coal. Neighbours will be the first to know when children wander the streets or are left alone at home. They may also have unrecognized friendships with a child which are a source both of assessment and help.

The family has a unique contribution to make in their knowledge of the child. They will have a view of the child shared by no-one else which will have *the* critical influence on the outcome of a child abuse investigation. It might even be argued that children are not problems as much as other people's perceptions of them. Those perceptions will contain vital clues not only about causes but also outcomes once an investigation is under way. Children do not exist in social isolation, it is their interactions with others which form the core of the social worker's assessment and the contact with the immediate carers is where the most important knowledge is located. The family will contribute to the investigation *directly* in their account of the child and *indirectly* through their interactions with him/her.

It is important that social workers are aware that knowledge about children exists in various forms, to different extents and at different locations. These sources are best seen as parts of the overall jigsaw of a comprehensive assessment and the wise worker will want to find them and fit them together. Thus an allegation, say, of inappropriate sexual behaviour to a child may need to be checked out not only with a paediatrician but also the school and the extended family. Access to a range of resources will reduce the amount of specialized child knowledge needed by a social worker; thus it may not matter if the significance of bruises is not known as long as the worker has quick access to someone who does; the extent of skill here would be a general alertness and a practised unease about a situation.

On this basis social workers do not need to be *experts* on child development, on specific signs and symptoms of abuse or on effective therapies for victims. If they wish to pursue these particular areas they run the risk of losing their unique oversight skills of the child-care process, or there are opportunities for specializations outside the statutory sector where much expert work is done. But if an expert status is either necessary nor possible within the limits of basic training what *do* social workers need to know about children? What will enable them to develop and practice the 'general alertness' mentioned above?

Categorizing knowledge about children

Earlier we used the idea of the social worker's child-care process as a way of locating external sources and types of knowledge. We can re-use this model again (Table 6.2) to consider the necessary knowledge for social workers at different stages. Ideally the model should be expressed in a circular three-dimensional way for two reasons: first, the process is not always linear; thus a knowledge of child abuse will greatly influence reactions to the initial referral. Secondly, the different areas of knowledge are all available continuously for the worker to draw on so that even while concentrated listening to the child will dominate an investigation the worker will be using a backdrop of experience of other similar children; or again concern about a lack of substitute care resources and the consequences will affect the assessment and decisions.

Consequences

It makes a lot of sense to begin by considering the effects on children of abuse. The whole growth of concern in this area is consequences-driven through the death of individual children, gross deprivation or system abuse

Table 6.2

Phase	Social work knowledge needed
Referral ↓	To evaluate the information in terms of *social and individual contexts* for children and in terms of *consequences* of similar abuse.
Investigation ↓	To listen to and *communicate* with children. To appreciate the *impact of the investigation* on children. To interpret children's *interactions* with their families. To look for *indicators* of abuse. To appreciate the *forensic* and *'therapeutic'* aspects of interviewing children. To understand what *inhibits* or *prevents* children from *divulging* abuse.
Assessment and decisions ↓	To evaluate *'significant harm'* or *'in need'* in terms of children's *physical, cognitive and emotional* development and needs. To evaluate protective and dangerous relationships for children. To *predict* the impact on children of *various outcomes*. To anticipate the children's *reactions* to decisions.
Consequences ↓	To monitor the effects of *substitute care* on children. To appreciate the *continuing importance* to children of the *families*. To understand the *initial and long-term consequences* of particular forms of abuse. To be aware of possible methods of help and treatment for victims of abuse.

through inappropriate intervention. Awareness of consequences should also enable social workers to categorize, where:

> The principal function of categorization, therefore, is to provoke an instant, detailed, and comprehensive conceptual framework in response to the term 'child [sexual] abuse' to facilitate the necessary differentiation amongst its many types and component parts. (O'Hagan, 1989, p. 64)

Thus we use a knowledge of consequences to underpin all other aspects of the child-care process.

Types of consequence

We need to distinguish between children feeling abused and being abused. Thus children may grow up in families 'isolated with little opportunity of observing no alternative family models' and may assume that their experiences are common (Doyle, 1990, p. 11). Their *relative* feeling of being badly treated may therefore be restricted and this can apply to individuals being abused by their carers *and* to whole categories of children who suffer socio-economic deprivation. Despite this the abuse will have consequences even though in some cases, the child's perception may come later.

Bradshaw's 'taxonomy of need' into felt, expressed, comparative and normative need (1977) is useful here so that the various aspects of abuse consequences can be disentangled. *Felt* need will be internal to the victim and may be difficult to tease out, if ever; or it may be *expressed* in different forms, either directly as a cry of complaint and anguish, or indirectly through damaged development or displaced or even sublimated behaviour. *Comparative* need can be assessed by investigating how abused children compare with others although the methodological problems here are considerable (see Browne and Finkelhor, 1986, ch. 5; Calam and Franchi, 1987; Dingwall, 1989, ch. 2; Kenward and Hevey, 1989, ch. 23).

Finally, abuse may be judged in *normative* terms because of value positions of professionals, the state or society whatever the actual consequences might be. This taxonomy will be used again in the following discussions.

If we leave aside the most extreme cases of child abuse caused by starvation, violent assault or gross denial of human rights it is not possible to provide neat summaries of consequences. At best the literature can only provide a *flavour*, through clinical accounts, survivors' stories or imperfect comparative research of what can happen to children who are abused. The wise worker will read as much of the literature as possible because although hard evidence is rarely available this does not invalidate findings as much as make their significance uncertain.

Contributions which offer models for estimating possible consequences are especially valuable. Browne and Finkelhor (1986, ch. 6) suggest, for sexual abuse, factors described as 'traumagenic dynamics' which can help to analyse the *experience* of the abuse (i.e. the felt need). These are:

Traumatic sexualization whereby the child's sexual development and attitudes become distorted so that later social integration and personal relationships are harmed. The effects are likely to be greater if the child is actively involved rather than allowed to be a passive victim and worse if the child is older and has more understanding of what is happening.

Betrayal as it suggests, reflects the victim's sense of being let down or tricked and of being left alone and without support or understanding. This is more likely if the offender is within the family but the authors make the further point that a sense of betrayal can also arise where the offender is a stranger *if* the parents do not act protectively or caringly enough. The converse is also true, of course, so that children may in fact survive better along this dimension if they do not feel betrayed. Although it relates to physical abuse the story of Azaro the spirit child in Ben Okri's novel *The Famished Road* (1991) illustrates this. Azaro, growing up in desperate poverty in rural Africa is sometimes beaten severely by his father but never indicates a sense of betrayal and indeed looks to him for continual love, security and pride.

Powerlessness 'refers to the process in which the child's will, desires and sense of efficacy are continually contravened' (p. 183). Physical force may not be necessary, it could equally be intense verbal entrapment or warnings about the consequences of resistance or 'telling'. The powerlessness can, of course, be made even worse if no one listens to or attends to the child although conversely, escape from the situation can reduce the effect.

Stigmatization leads children to feel increasingly different and deviant from others if they are sexually abused. This may then be compounded when other people do actually discriminate against the victim and treat him/her awkwardly or critically. On the other hand, sympathy and empathy may reduce this feeling and mutual help groups of victims can be important in this process.

This fourfold model may be open to some conceptual and empirical criticisms but it does provide frameworks built on the author's wide clinical and research experience. Beyond this, workers need to up-date their reading continually for reviews and re-reviews of current views about the effects of abuse. A recent publication is usefully set within the context of the Children Act and contains a useful discussion by Bentovim (1991, pp. 29–60).

While it may be possible to relate knowledge fragments to models as Browne and Finkelhor believe, attempts to relate particular consequences to specific types of abuse have not generally been successful. Not all battered children become timid or aggressive and not all sexually abused children have evident disturbances in their later sexual development. What may be more likely to suffer is their day-to-day functioning within their families and later in their own adult relationships.

Thorman (1982, ch. 2) offers a 'family functioning analysis' which explores interactions in terms of *power structure, autonomy, communication patterns* and *negotiation patterns*. For many of the children with whom social workers are involved it is in these areas that the consequences of abuse may be evident. How much power is the child given or able to achieve and are there any unusual power alliances in the family? How autonomous is the child especially with increasing age and is his/her identity and independence being confirmed? How well can the child communicate with others in the family and do any deficits suggest physical as well as social causes? Finally, how competently can the child negotiate in the wider sense? In a healthy situation family members will have the confidence to discuss issues and disgreements; a child who has difficulty doing this may be undermined by a deep pessimism or despair born of betrayal or powerlessness. Whatever the constellation of abuse consequences a wide social assessment can sometimes provide as many clues as expert diagnoses.

In-care and consequences

Research into the effects of being in substitute care is well established in the UK and has had the benefit of being less buffeted by changes in definition than the general child abuse field. Works referred to in previous chapters (DHSS, 1985; Kahan, 1989; DoH, 1991e, and see also Aldgate and Simmonds, 1988, chs 1 and 3) have shown that children come into care at a disadvantage and may suffer further reverses. The pressures on, and shortage of foster parents and the lack of qualified staff in residential care can produce children who, having been separated from their families do not always receive sufficient compensation. Their difficulties may be reflected in the high incidence of in-care children amongst runaways.

The position of children of ethnic minorities at the hands of the professional and care system may be especially acute. Maximé (1986) gives a clinical psychologist's account of the painful identity and adjustment problems faced by black children and Lau (1991, pp. 101–14) offers vivid examples of the effects of culturally insensitive assessments on children and their families. We have previously referred to the particular threats to black teenagers at the hands of the criminal justice system which may leave them criminalized and less able in their turn to establish secure and successful families of their own.

This account of the consequences of abuse in the wide sense can only outline areas for study. Lewels of abuse vary greatly and the dynamics of the abuse event or episode (whether hours or years) will contribute unique elements. Social workers will need to weigh up factors like initial or long-term effects, possible hidden feelings about abuse as well as visible effects, whether some forms of abuse will be more vulnerable to further harm within the care system, whether family placement will be emotionally inappropriate and those aspects of suffering which are more redeemable than others.

Referral knowledge

As we suggested, at the point of referral the social worker brings wide experience and knowledge to bear about how *this particular* alleged abuse could end up. In addition it will be necessary to put the allegation into some kind of context and priority system. Not all forms of abuse could or should be responded to and our earlier example of Azaro the spirit boy in Africa is again relevant. Paternal beatings, in fact a high level of violence, were common in his society and so his particular situation would have been unremarkable to his fellows.

The knowledge needed here concerns cultural and sub-cultural norms, neighbourhood circumstances and local concerns. How do families and children behave in a particular area and are these generally accepted? It is here that awareness of differing ethnic minority values will be important although this then raises the issue of 'cultural relativism' (see Stevenson, 1989, pp. 197–203 for a summary of this in relation to child abuse). This refers to the dilemma about where, in society, to establish a basis for deciding what is acceptable treatment of children. Discussions of cultural relativism have focused mostly on ethnic minorities but it has class application too. The social worker needs some appreciation of such issues so that any referral about child abuse will be treated as rationally as possible. The sources of knowledge may well be community and religious figures who may have important information about child-rearing patterns in particular neighbourhoods. Such knowledge does not 'let the social worker off the hook'; the stream of official inquiries in the last twenty years reveal, if nothing else, that society is far from clear about the treatment of children and social workers' tasks symbolize this uncertainty.

This approach reflects the ecological view of children and families that we used in Chapter Four. Garbarino (1982) set out this model in detail in order to consider families and their environment and uses the term 'The Child's Turf' (ch. 7) to explore the way children need to be set within a developmental social context. Social workers may not always use such knowledge consciously but it clearly influences initial reactions to allegations.

Investigation knowledge

It is during the investigation phase in allegations of individual abuse that the greatest pressure and focus arises for the social worker. The task is a double one: to carry out a legal protective investigation while working within social work values and frameworks. This requires that the worker recognizes that the context affects the necessary communication with the child. This means that the child who is the client may also suffer from the pressure of the investigation especially where sexual abuse is suspected. The evidence which emerges from the Orkney Inquiry may crystallize this important issue and perhaps generate fresh guidelines and precautions. Before then, material from PAIN and from the Cleveland Inquiry reveal that children can be at risk from heavy-handed investigations.

Insights into children's perceptions and reactions are available from several sources. Faller (1988, ch. 7) explores the process of the interview in sexual abuse and a range of verbal and non-verbal approaches and techniques which include the use of anatomically explicit dolls. Glaser and Frosh (1988) discuss investigation issues at length and interweave legal and process issues with the needs of the child (especially pp. 88–100). Wells (1989, ch. 3) suggests that good interviewing in sexual abuse cases depends on appreciating children's general social relationships to adults and the problems of power. Thus:

> To get better at this complex task [of communicating with children], made more difficult by our collective historical traditions, practitioners have to enter the vulnerable world where these children have been, where they continue to be, and where adults come from. (p. 52)

In the same work Glasgow (1989, ch. 9) looks at the value of play-based assessments and concludes with a useful list of 'Common Mistakes'.

It is inevitable that the particular problems of interviewing children who may have been sexually abused have generated proportionately much more material than other forms of abuse. A forthcoming book by O'Hagan (1992) will focus on emotional abuse and like his previous book on sexual abuse (1989) draws heavily on case examples and children's perceptions. Although Doyle's writing (1990) is concerned with children after they have been abused it has much throughout that is appropriate to investigation work. The third chapter, aptly entitled *Voices of the Children*, includes reflective accounts of abuse which give direct access to the victims' thoughts, feelings and language about their experiences. This book also contains a fund of practice wisdom and suggestions for working with children.

Are children 'truthful?'

We have already referred at various points in this book to the pressures created by current concerns about child abuse and especially allegations of sexual abuse. The effect has been, at times, to pitch inexperienced social workers into intimate and intensive interviews with children. The Cleveland Inquiry expressed its clear view about the dangers that can arise; related to this is the question of evaluating what children say. Are they truthful when they allege or admit abuse, are they accurate, do they get confused or, even, do they tell lies?

Common sense tells us that just as adults sometimes need to be untruthful so might children. The three key considerations would seem to be age, motives and pressures. Although evidence is not widespread a recent National Children's Bureau/Barnardos paper (1991) has a useful summary of knowledge about *Children as Witnesses* expressed thus:

> Children are nowadays thought to be no more (and no less) likely than adults to tell deliberate lies.

> Like adults, children do not tell lies without some motive or reason; there is no truth in the theory that children invent false allegations of sexual abuse without either.

Children who try to tell the truth are no less credible than adults on the ground that their memories are weaker; in so far as they have greater trouble in remembering, the tendency is to leave things out rather than accidentally to invent what did not happen.

However, for various reasons, children more readily produce incorrect information in the face of overbearing questioning than do adults.

When trying to make sense of what a child says, or to understand his or her motive for saying it, it is important to try to see the matter through the eyes of the child.

Faller (1988, pp. 126–34) also explores, with case examples, 'untrue' sexual allegations by children. She identifies 'social desirability' as a reason why children may make statements particularly if they feel that their questioners or other adults are looking for such admissions. Deliberately false accusations are very unlikely by young children although older children may make them but often because they already have a degree of emotional damage. Faller also makes the important point that the untruths may be in the other direction when children either deny known abuse or later retract admissions for complex motives.

Wakefield and Underwager (1988, ch. 12) discuss the general issue of false sexual abuse accusations and, in their review of American literature, point to a more complex picture especially in parental relationship breakdown; here children may come under intense pressure to side with one parent against the other and this may produce statements which are consciously *or* unconsciously false. In such situations the social worker (and the police) will need to make a full social assessment which identifies possible pressure points on children and motives they may have to say one thing rather than another. What does seem unarguable is that, except in the case of older teenagers, even if statements are unreliable they will have been made for good reason and this itself is cause for concern about family relationships.

Assessment knowledge

Athough assessment is implied in the investigation phase it will inevitably be incomplete. Often the full review of evidence will come later at a case conference. The social worker may have access to specialist assessments of a child but makes a vital contribution by co-ordinating and appraising the comments of others. This is a *legal* duty in line with the requirements of the Children Act 1989. That legislation defines *significant harm* and *in need*, not only in terms of specific acts of ill-treatment but more broadly against a developmental background set down in Sections 17 and 31.

The Act clearly expects that assessments will be made about a particular child's state of development and this is therefore an important area of knowledge for social workers. As we argued earlier in this chapter it would not be possible or appropriate for them to become experts in this wide field but they need an overall awareness of physical, cognitive and emotional development in children and there are welcome signs that this need is being better addressed both in basic and later training. The learning is greatly enhanced by direct observation of children and the recent CCETSW publication *The Teaching of Child Care in the Diploma in Social Work* (1991a) provides a helpful framework for designing such activities.

The CCETSW book has also commissioned excellent papers (chs 10 and 11) on the three aspects of child development; these are detailed and comprehensive and come with extensive bibliographies. Particularly welcome are sections on ethnicity and gender as well as mental and physical handicap. Because this material was specially commissioned it is tuned to the needs of social workers. The Department of Health, *Protecting Children* (DoH, 1988) is also written for social workers as an aid to assessment. It devotes a section (8.2) to children's behaviour and development and includes the well-known Sheridan developmental charts. The guide has a strong individual flavour and although there is reference to social networks and the inclusion of an *ecomap*, the ecological perspective is not strong; this is particularly true of the bibliography which is limited and selective.

A book of this nature could not begin to summarize children's development. Support for social workers and the knowledge available to them is growing as we have indicated but any assessment must always be multi-disciplinary and *Working Together* makes this clear. This should not be restricted to professional 'experts' as may happen in an area of work which has become more formal and legalistic. Parents, relatives, friends and neighbours can all contribute valuable information about children's developmental histories and present patterns and the opening out of case conferences will make this more possible. Government guidelines regarding the new Child Assessment Orders acknowledge the continuing role of parents both directly and via second opinions, an issue which has been a major concern of PAIN.

Decision knowledge

This matter requires brief discussion. It begs the question of how social workers are to ascertain the wishes and feelings of children as required by the Children Act. The concern to protect children should not have the effect of diminishing them as people. The child-care process can easily acquire an official momentum that drags children with it. *Working Together* says in paragraph 6: 13:

Whenever children have sufficient understanding and are able to express their wishes and feelings *and to participate in the process of investigation, assessment, planning and review*, they should be encouraged to attend conferences. (italics added)

and:

Equally the professional who is working most closely with a child should keep the child informed about the decisions and recommendations reached at the conference and any changes in the inter-agency plan.

To do this the worker will need to communicate skilfully with the child as more than a potential witness or merely a victim. Research has frequently suggested that helplessness is a serious consequence of abuse; if this is true then any intervention which shifts the child from passive to active is to be encouraged. This work will be easier to achieve if the worker has some understanding of how children themselves perceive their abuse (and this may differ from the worker's view), the people or situations which abuse them, and how they hope it will be resolved. What this amounts to, by way of summarizing this section is that knowledge about children is not something to be applied in a cold clinical fashion to abuse situations. Rather it is something to be brought to the assessment, negotiation and planning process in child care.

Summary

In this chapter we have focused on social workers' contact with children. We began with a note of caution about the demands made on statutory workers in child protection and pointed out the still inadequate realities of training both before and after qualification. The child care field has expanded considerably in the glare of the publicity surrounding child abuse inquiries and this creates great pressure on the statutory services.

I have used a model of the child-care process to think about and locate knowledge about children. Such knowledge in partial form is held by a wide range of people both professionally and informally and I include parents, families and local networks. Nevertheless, social workers themselves require a sound knowledge base about children. Some of the literature, models and approaches available have been reviewed briefly and I have commended recent publications from the DoH and CCETSW which are designed specially for social workers.

The chapter ends, rightly, with children themselves. The child protection process has an in-built tendency to operate will-nilly as a package *imposed* by professionals *on* children. This is potentially, and sometimes actually, abusive; it needs monitoring and the new Children Act acknowledges this through its central and constant emphasis on consulting children. This theme provides the appropriate base for the final chapter which will bring together the themes identified thus far and attempt some speculations about the future for children in relation to the state and to social workers.

7 / THE FUTURE

Tomorrow's social context

Previous chapters have identified and explored a number of themes that impinge on our thinking about child abuse: history, social unease, affluence, recession, moral panic, child protection, services to families, children's rights, partnership with parents, the law, the state of knowledge and the position of social work. These themes will reappear in this final chapter which speculates about the future for children and how they might be helped by the state both directly and indirectly through its agents. What should be evident is that child abuse only makes sense if we try to understand its social background; the last twenty years reveal dramatic changes in emphasis whether regarding definitions of child-care policy and practice. The political background as a distinct aspect of society also has a key role and at the time of writing, it is impossible to anticipate whether major shifts in ideology lie ahead; what seems likely is that no present-day government will make radical changes in child-care policy because of pressing economic and tactical problems.

The anxious society

In Chapter 2 use was made of Harding's four perspectives (1991) as a way of interpreting child-care policy and legislation. Although her conclusions are that the present position represents 'an uneasy synthesis' (ch. 7) it is also clear that state intervention is now well established. Partly, this reflects a modern world which has shrunk because information technology brings everyone closer and thus easier to label and monitor. The growth of European Community influence is likely to accelerate this process by emphasizing the interdependence of social and economic units within and between members. More sophisticated and powerful data collection casts light into more dark corners of which childhood is especially important.

Intervention is not just an accidental result of information technology. It also reflects moral and political concerns which come in two forms. First, child-care policy and legislation may stem from a positive normative belief that *all* children need a minimum level of care and services to achieve a quality of life. This characterized the universalistic social democratic perspective in the UK from 1945 to the mid-1970s. This was a largely optimistic concern with children in general expressed through expanding state provision. The second form is more pessimistic and cost-conscious; it identifies particular areas of child care as problematic and needing special attention. This perspective has dominated the last fifteen years of policy and practice with protection becoming the crucial focus of state social work. Although the new Children Act appears to restore some balance our analysis questions this particularly in the context of current politics and the severe shortage of money for services.

Protection concerns mirror widespread anxieties in society which are discussed briefly in Chapter 1. Developments in the UK (and the USA) in the last twenty years could be taken as a lesson to less developed countries that affluence does not eliminate social unease. Erich Fromm (1978) has distinguished between 'Having' and 'Being', suggesting that modern materialistic societies are preoccupied with the first; this tends to reduce life to 'object' transactions and undermine social and moral relationships. Anxiety rises in this climate through a fear of losing possessions. Materialism also makes sharp distinctions between those who have things and those who don't with the former group devoting ever more time and worry to protecting what they have.

If the 1950s and 1960s were characterized by the sprouting of television aerials on houses, the 1980s equivalent is burglar and car alarms in a society where more than 90 per cent of crimes are committed against property. Gortz' concept (see Chapter 1) of a new 'non-class of non-workers' describes a growing amorphous social group of people who are not identified with traditional work and consumer ethics. They represent another source of anxiety for society and a possible threat to society. Major economic changes in the 1980s have been accompanied by well-documented shifts in attitudes towards gender and family roles. In some parts of society these changes are in their infancy but they will continue to grow producing their own pressures on children. We may be at a very stressful transitional point where the traditional family is in decline but before the social infrastructure has developed for whatever may replace it. The practical effect is a rise in hard-pressed lone parent–child relationships or complex re-constituted family structures.

Pre-occupation with rights

Jordan (1990, p. 85) has talked of rights as 'exclusion zones' granted to individuals to keep other people out. The Children Act 1989 emphasizes and incorporates many such rights – to protect parents from an intrusive state, and a child from abusive parents for example. This has also been a prominent political theme in recent years in the shape of rights for patients, buyers of goods, watchers of television advertisements, ferry passengers, people under arrest, ethnic minorities, women, and for citizens in general. Although the provisions may be sometimes framed as rights *to* rather than protection *from* something they all indicate a social unease that things need putting right. However, as Jordan argues this concept of rights has the effect of fencing people off. Although his particular focus is the relationship between families and child protection workers, his more general theme is that the emphasis on rights implies 'an adversarial situation' in 'a culture of antagonism' (p. 91) which, we argue, characterizes wider social relationships. Such a culture diminishes the role of co-operation and negotiation.

To give rights to one person means to hold someone else to account and this is a striking feature of modern society. Whether a ferry boat sinks, a football crowd is crushed or a child dies inquiries seek to lay blame. Where before we invoked 'Act of God' we now look for culprits closer at hand. While it is wrong not to acknowledge the value of the rights movement it has to be understood within prevailing social moods and if these are anxiety and fear then the consequences may inhibit rather than promote social relationships.

Hall and colleagues' (1978) analysis of moral panic illustrates the difficulties; later terms such as 'authoritarian populism' (Hall, 1980) and 'consensual authoritarianism' (Norrie and Adelman, 1989) sharpen our view of a social anxiety which leads to adversarial and harsh policies. These pander to popular fears by offering acceptable but partial and short-term solutions. As we argued in Chapter 1 it is this process which may partly account for the extraordinary hostility towards social workers. For this reason the new Children Act's balancing act may fail if it owes more to well-intentioned civil servants and lawyers' logic than to popular and political moods.

The promotion of rights in isolation may serve merely to sharpen appetites and increase resentment. Children's rights illustrate this well. It seems possible that the Children Act will raise awareness, creating fresh demands on parents and on the state through its domiciliary services and substitute care. For parents the increased accountability will not fall evenly. Families who are already under pressure from discrimination or poverty will be less able to respond to their children's demands than better-off parents. Local authority services which are under-funded and/or under-qualified will find their weaknesses more exposed than ever. It could be argued that this is one of the functions of a rights movement, to reveal inequalities, but there has also to be a reasonable possibility of 'delivering' those rights.

Public reaction to events in Cleveland, Rochdale and Orkney further illustrate the dilemmas of the rights movement. Inquiries before 1988 gave a clear impression that children's 'right' to protection was being attended to by the state via its social services. The events in question which were easily predictable within a moral panic analysis, shocked the public into realizing that the problem had not gone away; yet the moral panic process is still not exhausted, official findings continue to focus on social work rather than society and to insist that children's rights must be addressed in an isolated legalistic fashion.

Protection or promotion

Will current trends in state child-care work continue? The answer may depend on wider social movements in the future. In Chapter 1 Western social affluence was related to 'higher-order' concerns in abuse about emotional suffering rather than physical ill-treatment and based on a widespread view that individual cases were more dangerous than socio-economic conditions.

The future of child-care work could go in several directions. If the economic recession eases, higher-order concerns will continue and services to families may benefit enough for action to be directed at child abuse on different fronts as the Children Act assumes. Protection will be exercised firmly and fairly with due respect for family privacy, by reasonably funded services staffed by better trained workers. However, if the economic recovery unleashes the kind of materialistic explosion witnessed in the mid-1980s as part of an anti-collective individualism the darker side of consumer choice will threaten promotion. It will be assumed that in a land of renewed opportunity the 'losers' must bear considerable personal responsibility especially if they are parents. A residual model of child care will expect much of voluntary and private efforts and create wide inequalities in service levels.

If the economic recession does not ease, services for children will decline more quickly than expectations and the rights movement. Will this also mean a shift from higher-order to lower-order concerns about child abuse? Will we be too preoccupied with earning a living to worry about children's 'developmental' and 'autonomy' interests? Will we see a decline in reports about sexual or ritual abuse?

Although a severe and *widespread* decline in living standards would have a dramatic effect on child-care concerns this would not be immediate. The time-lag of expectations might, instead, aggravate discontentment and heighten the search for scapegoats. In such a situation the most visible offenders would be gravely exposed and this means poor people already known to child protection services. An important paradox of the growth in higher-order concerns is that it has had little substantial effect on the socio-economic picture of social services clients. 'Child sexual abuse is no respecter of class or race' (Search, 1988, p. 15) but it might be added 'except in social services case lists'. This would again enable the complex socio-psychological process whereby child abuse anxieties result in increased pressure on social workers. Except in a powerful climate of puritanism we are not likely to see any *cross-sectional* rooting out of abuse, only an increase in surveillance of poor families.

The 'snatch squad'

Harsh times could lead to harsh measures. Present child protection work already contains the seeds of oppression and these could flourish in suitable conditions. Until around 1970 NSPCC workers were called Inspectors, wore uniforms and were widely known as 'The Cruelty Men'. It was their absorption into a more enlightened child-care service which made this image inappropriate and uncomfortable. A continuing recession might put the clock back by firmly separating protection from promotion work with dangerous consequences for social workers and families.

A perceptive article in *Social Work Today* (23/11/89) looks ahead to 2018, the fiftieth anniversary of the Seebohm Report which led to the creation of Social Services Departments. It imagines a new service:

> Built on the nucleus of the old NSPCC child protection units, the new network of rescue units made up the new National Child Rescue Service. Each Unit consisted of five police officers, two doctors, two social workers and a health visitor. Armed with the powers given them in the 1999 Child Rescue Act, the Rescue Units were heralded as the ultimate child abuse deterrent. (p. 37)

It turns the screw with further descriptions of repealed sex discrimination legislation in order to recruit all-male teams, national computer data-bases for families, 230-item checklists of child abuse symptoms and the provision for removing children without court orders! Sadly, the article was anonymous but its predictions are not so fanciful that they can be dismissed lightly.

We have previously commented on the legalism of present child protection work and on the close collaboration between police and social workers. The fact that this goes largely unremarked upon in present social work literature (unlike in the early 1970s) indicates how important principles and attitudes can change incrementally. In the USA there is occasional evidence of very tough measures against errant parents. A Charleston, North Carolina scheme allows police to arrest mothers if there is concern about care of their children because of drug problems; the mothers are placed in compulsory rehabilitation programmes with the risk of subsequent prison if they are on cocaine or heroin and do not co-operate (BBC 1, 'Everyman' Programme, 19/1/92). Thus the potential will exists to develop more extreme forms of child protection.

Local authority social services are on the verge of major re-organization because of care in the community legislation. If this is implemented it will further the division between care management with assessment and provision of services. If a climate and structure develops where skilled services are provided *outside* of local authority Social Services Departments this could affect staff recruitment. How attractive would a residual state child-care service be? What would its functions and methods be?

While it is not yet clear whether child-care services could or would follow the patterns for adult services, it would be concerning if the local authority setting generally proved to be less attractive to qualified social workers. American experience does not suggest that state child care offers a consistent, nationwide quality service to the most vulnerable families. It is therefore important that current UK debates about local authority service reorganization take account of wider child-care issues.

In the last chapter we talked in ecological terms of the Exosystem; this was a system which impinges on children and families over which they have little or no influence. It was suggested that statutory child care is such a system but that it can become permeable to some extent. The extent of this permeability is a crucial issue. A harsh apparatus of 'Rescue Units' would not be permeable at all and this would objectify not only parents but also the children who were being rescued. Edward's story in Chapter 5 suggests the way protection work might too readily dismiss partnership; this has the effect of not allowing connections between the family system and the formal professional system.

The dilemmas for social workers themselves are profound. The optimism and sometimes reckless expansionism of the late 1960s and early 1970s may well have left some children unprotected and the Maria Colwell case was an important reminder of this. Since then, skilled and committed protection work has confronted uncomfortable illusions about 'happy families', brought light to dark places and improved the lives of many children. At some point, perhaps this movement peaked and since then, as we have tried to argue, returns have been diminishing both for children and for social workers themselves. This raises the question of how some kind of ethical and practical compromise might be achieved and this is the last theme in this book.

A child-care dialogue

First Love Last Rites is a collection of stories by the novelist Ian McEwan (1976). The first of these, *Homemade*, is an account of teenage male sexuality and includes an explicit description of a 14 year-old boy who persuades his innocent ten year-old sister to allow him to have intercourse with her. In many ways it is a classic example of sexual abuse: the initiating male sex drive, the soft words and the deception, the betrayal of trust, the naive victim and the opportunity caused by the parents' temporary absence.

If social workers became aware of this incident how should they react to it? They would certainly be informed by a feminist analysis of the way so many 'normal' males can commit sexual abuse and indeed the boy in the story does not seem at all unusual. Much would depend on the parents' reactions once they became aware of the incident and on some kind of assessment of the boy. Had he done it before, was he likely to do it again, and was he under any outside influence? The picture is complicated because at one point in the seduction the boy fumbling until his sister with innocent impatience guides him; she then falls asleep only to wake up at the end and cry. McEwan's comment might serve as the basis for a social work assessment:

> This may have been one of the most desolate couplings known to copulating mankind, involving lies, deceit, humiliation [of the boy], incest, my partner falling asleep, my gnat's orgasm and the sobbing which now filled the bedroom. (p. 24)

Although this incident fits well with theorizing about sexual abuse *in general* it is nevertheless a unique encounter between two people and also illustrates the way literature outside of social work can provide valuable 'case' material. A narrow reaction from protection workers might see only the fact of the abuse, the assumed damage to the victim and the need to play safe because of the weight and demands of the law. However Jordan, in developing his earlier argument, sees risks here:

> Social workers come to see their duties as grounds for action or inaction which take no account of the client's experiences, projects or commitments, but only of their legal rights. This drains their encounter of most of its creative and helpful potential. It reduces it to a purely formal exchange. (1990, p. 103)

The 'moral content' he refers to is perhaps to be found in the values which should inform social work and give it a distinctive character. For Jordan this involves developing the kind of ethics which arise from respect for persons and a willingness to communicate and negotiate. This is no easy task because social work occupies an unusual position and there is a continuing debate, as was identified in Chapter 3, about the extent to which social workers have an identity outside of their statutory duties and settings (see Horne, 1987, part 3). The essence of the dilemma is that a person's moral identity will depend on their becoming clients of social workers, but this per se turns them into *objects*. Good assessment, on the other hand, requires that we understand people subjectively.

In McEwan's story the subjective state of the ten year-old girl is very important. She is not merely an object of theorizing and law but also a person who, in this case, only 'consented' to be abused because her brother agreed to spend quite a long time playing her favourite game of 'Mummies and Daddies'. It would only be through 'a dialogue between client and worker'

(Jordan, 1990, p. 93) that the 'facts' of the encounter could be established and a proper plan made.

Elements of open assessment

Aldgate (1991, pp. 6–10) suggests the same kind of ecological approach to partnership that was explored in Chapter 6. She argues that individuals whether clients or not need to be seen 'as resources which can be marshalled' (p. 9) taking account of their total environment. On this basis our ten year-old girl is more than just a victim and it might well be sufficient within the family to work with her to boost her otherwise secure role in relation to her older brother so that she can rebuff him in future. The boy himself, understood in relation to male socialization as well as his own development needs help to understand that sisters are off-limits. The parents may need advice about how pubescent boys tend to behave, to reinforce the above themes. What is essential is that all the family members as individuals and within their microsystems are brought into the assessment in an active way.

A good assessment will make use of both predisposing and situational factors in building up a risk analysis (Cooper and Ball, 1987, ch. 4). A guide which contains both elements is offered by Stein and Rzepnicki (1983, pp. 60–61):

1 There is no adult willing to care for a child, or the child refuses to stay in the home.
2 There is medical evidence that physical abuse or nutritional neglect is so severe as to be life-threatening.
3 There was intent to kill the child, even if injury is not severe. Medical evidence should support a hypothesis of deliberate poisoning, or marks on the child's body should indicate assault with a deadly weapon or repeated beating with a heavy object.
4 There is medical or psychological evidence of abuse or neglect that, without medical intervention, may threaten the child's life, *and* the parent refuses help.
5 Medical evidence of repeated abuse exists. This reference is to previous untreated injuries, generally identified through X-rays, where the location or type of injury suggests prior maltreatment.
6 Severe abuse or neglect recurs after services were offered.
7 Severe emotional abuse or neglect is evidenced by behavioural disturbance or withdrawal by the child, *and* the parent rejects the child.
8 Medical or psychological evidence suggests that the parent is incompetent to provide minimum child care and there are no resources (e.g. family, friends, or community services) to help in the home while assessment is under way.

9 A child has been raped by a related adult or a non-related adult known to the parent, *and* the parent did not attempt to protect the child.

Their systematic study and review suggest that the presence of one or more of the above factors would be good reason for removing a child from home.

Faller (1988, ch. 10) also offers a useful chapter on case management in sexual abuse with a 'decision-making matrix' (p. 269) which evaluates parents and their relationships; a key factor is the position of the non-abusing parent in relation to the perpetrator and the victim and especially the ability to act independently to protect the latter. Finkelhor's (1984) *Four Pre-Conditions Model* of sexual abuse also combines predisposing and situational factors. While locating responsibility firmly with the abuser it shows how outcomes depend on the dynamic interaction of events and individuals. Even so, although Finkelhor's model is invaluable in identifying the elements in a process it still begs certain moral questions that need a dialogue in Jordan's terms. As we saw in McEwan's story, both children brought their own complex histories, personalities and prior relationship into their encounter and this must not be neglected.

If the social work assessment of McEwan's encounter was that the girl was likely to suffer significant harm in the future there is still considerable incentive to prevent her coming into state care. A proper risk analysis might indicate that further sexual abuse was not the only danger. O'Hagan's (1989, ch. 6) discussions about the dangers of removal of children from their families are relevant here and the Children Act in its checklist for courts considering whether to make orders on children, includes 'the likely effect on him of any change in his circumstances' (Section I(3)(C)).

The involved family

It makes both legal and social work sense to seek solutions outside of the formal substitute care system. New Zealand practitioners preparing for a conference on partnership in London organized by the Family Rights Group in November 1991, refer to research evidence that children are 'ten times as likely to be sexually abused in care as in their own family' (Smith, 1991, p. 20). His paper also describes methods which actively encourage the participation of extended family members in child-care decisions. It is acknowledged that the New Zealand situation is heavily influenced by strong Maori traditions about family ties but the commitment to informal solutions is generally applicable.

An ecological approach will attempt to identify the family's active microsystems in the hope that amongst them may be resources that can be utilized both for immediate protection to the child as well as longer term solutions. Malucchio et al. (1986) provide detailed guidance for such an approach and offer a crucial rationale for involving parents, for if they feel powerless they:

> can hold onto these feelings as a way of exonerating themselves. When one has no power in a situation or a decision, one cannot be held accountable. The attitude that 'the system will do what it wants anyway' allows the parent to feel victimized and, in a sense, innocent. (p. 146)

Although extended families may not be the resource they once were parents should be encouraged to consider them. Even in long-term foster care relatives appear to be significantly more successful than stranger placements (Rowe et al., 1984) and the importance of the extended family is now beginning to be exploited in more open forms of adoption.

Wider initiatives

A network approach to assessment and planning will connect the family to various systems both formal and informal. Holman, who has maintained an incurable optimism, compassion and commitment to prevention suggests that help is sometimes more effective if families in trouble are put in touch with 'normal' neighbourhood resources rather than provided with special facilities.

Holman investigated a number of preventive projects run by the Children's Society and identified three different models (1988, ch. 5). The *client-focused model* offered specialized services to particular client groups who were often referred by statutory bodies especially the social services department. The benefits were good quality staff, planned activities and the capacity to respond to crises. The disadvantages were that such a service could acquire a reputation as a centre for 'bad' families and would not be seen as belonging to or appealing to the community in general.

The *neighbourhood model* tended to offer a wider range of less expert services which were used by a mixture of local people including those known to statutory services. Holman saw the greater community involvement as the main strength of this model although it was less easily managed because of its multiple functions. As well it was reported that social services departments were less happy to give general financial backing to people who were not normally their clients.

The third *community development model* differed from the previous one in following community work principles more closely. It emphasized the central organizing role for local people rather than paid staff and a greater focus on collective action and goals. As a result there was less willingness to undertake individual work or become too closely involved with statutory bodies. Holman acknowledges that this model is the most difficult of the three to sustain in its pure form and it tends to need the security of sound financial backing from outside bodies. It also seems likely that political tensions will be a greater problem with this model and this creates real difficulties for statutory agencies who are accountable for spending public money.

Holman's study and his more general advocacy of neighbourhood initiatives deserve study. We have pointed to the danger of protection services becoming closed exosystems and this militates against a partnership approach. Unfortunately, the Children Act 1989 is at its weakest in its pronouncements about community integration and prevention. Where it refers to a mixed economy its market philosophy seems to colour its language and the lack of specific funding does not encourage radical initiatives in partnership. On the other hand the Act's political base does anticipate that statutory agencies should be more willing to purchase services from whoever might have something to offer. This provides an incentive to voluntary projects to set out their wares in detail and make bids for contracts. This kind of discipline may be necessary for approaches which sometimes find clarity of purpose and structure a problem.

Gibbons' study (1990) of the involvement of a social services area team in a family support policy is a useful assessment of the kind of links which Holman advocates. The balance between client focus and neighbourhood models was not easy to achieve. The local authority social workers also faced dilemmas. Although they were often very knowledgeable about local resources, 'inexorable pressures from rising numbers of child abuse referrals prevented the implementation of even a modest switch of social work time towards community activities' (p. 160). As Gibbons indicates, involvement in wider community schemes raises important questions about social work functions and tasks and these in turn have implications for the way social services departments are organized. It is this issue of structuring which will be the last theme of this chapter.

Organizing for child care

Earlier in this chapter we speculated about how future social conditions might influence child-care services. What seems inescapable is that local authority social services departments do not have the professional or political power to determine their own fate. Even so important debates are imminent about how state services might be organized to provide good services for children. There are three key ingredients to these debates and these are the purchase/provision issue, possible local government boundary reorganization and, finally, discussions about setting up a general Social Work or Social Services Council.

Purchase and provision

We have referred to this issue at various points in this book and it therefore does not need much more explanation here. Present evidence, mostly informal from the working discussions of social services departments, suggests that child care is not easily divided up between those who make assessments and develop 'care plans' for clients and those who provide services whether they be initial protection, day-care, residential care or rehabilitation.

A split is difficult because, as was argued in Chapter 6, state social workers are involved in the whole child-care process and the parental role is clearly and comprehensively defined in legislation. At the same time, the last twenty years has shown the dominance of the residual model and so a split from some aspects of provision has occurred. This has left state social workers focusing mainly on investigation, assessment, substitute care and rehabilitation for the most vulnerable families. Other aspects of provision have been left to voluntary agencies for prevention and specialist treatment services especially for abused children. The work is often short term except where children come into compulsory care; here we may see the best mix of purchase and provision as social workers attempt complex rehabilitation plans with difficult and damaged families. This kind of work will become even more important because the Children Act's philosophy is that compulsory court orders such as adoption must be shown to offer opportunities for children not available elsewhere.

Clearly some child-care provisions are already separated from planning and assessment and this trend may well continue. Perhaps the important question is what remains the residual model; if it is only a narrow investigation and protection function that may have the worrying consequences we discussed earlier.

Local government boundary reorganization

The question of the appropriate size and shape of local government units is a perpetual topic for politicians. 1968 and 1974 last saw altered boundaries raising familiar debates about economy of scale versus remoteness and bureaucracy. What structures are likely to benefit children and families best? It would seem to depend on the preferred concept of the child-care service.

Large authorities can offer good career structures for social work staff, better opportunities for advanced training and specialization and the promotion of consistent services over a wide area. In a more favourable national political climate the leaders of large authority social services departments might be better able to fight for greater funds for child-care promotion and longer term targets. On the other hand, smaller units offer better local responsiveness to community needs. Because social workers would be less numerous, integration with other staff might occur more readily and this would appear to facilitate the kind of organization favoured by patch system advocates and community workers. Liaison between different parts of small authorities – social services, housing, health and planning – would encourage multi-faceted initiatives and the co-working of professional and para-professional staff. This also accords better with the demands of the rights movement for greater accountability of officials. Finally, the greater exposure of less numerous social workers would lead to more clarification of their role and tasks.

Overall, smaller local units could lead to systems which are more easily permeated whether by other disciplines, elected members or local communities. This might be especially beneficial for ethnic minorities where state services have, in the past, been accused of being too remote and too Eurocentric. Local structures might better promote formal and informal methods of working that deliver services which are more ethnically sensitive especially for children in substitute care. The greatest problems of localization are parochialism and inconsistent standards. Small authorities may be poorly resourced as well as isolated in terms of a child-care culture. An important factor in the Seebohm Committee's wish to create larger social services departments was sound evidence of enormous variations in child-care statistics about need and provision. A degree of uniformity is essential in children's services but the growth of the Social Services Inspectorate offers a way of monitoring local standards and laying down minimum standards. The provisions of the Children Act provide a strong foundation for this which did not exist in the past.

A social work council

In Chapter 3 the tension between elitism and egalitarianism which has underlain social work thinking since the 1960s was discussed. Are children and families best helped by a body of workers cast in the professional mould akin to doctors and lawyers? Such a body would have clear training and qualification standards, regulated entry and visible control by regulatory body; it would also, likely, have a more distinctive public image, a better defined domain of work and recognized specialist skills. Alternatively, social workers might be more characterized by a core of individualist/collective social principles but a more fluid range of skills that put a premium on permeability and multi-level collaboration.

These possibilities assume greater importance because of current debates at CCETSW level about the possible formation of some kind of national council that would have registration and regulation powers. The main issues are summarized in Parker's report *Safeguarding Standards* (1990) which concludes, first that social workers themselves now support such a council more than previously, and secondly that there is a good case for a council. He points in particular to child abuse inquiries and other events in the 1980s which have highlighted the issue of social work accountability.

Perhaps Parker's most significant recommendation is that any proposed council should not be restricted to qualified social workers but should incorporate other care staff within a 'General Social Services Council'. His main argument is a 'default' one, namely that as social workers form only a minority of social services staff the restricted model would be incomplete and would not meet public expectations. This would appear to align Parker firmly with theorists such as Howe (1986) who define social work in terms of the statutory employer context.

This is a complex issue which is beyond the scope of this book. It does, nevertheless, raise major questions again about the identity of social work. Would a possible amorphous definition of social work bring benefits to children and families or would it be a dangerous attack on its core values? It should be clear that this book favours a conception of social work that is more than a sum of techniques, skills and tasks but has an ethical base as Jordan proposes.

Safeguarding children

This has not been a book about children but about their position within a society which has adopted particular philosophies and methods of helping them. What children need is not easily understood because at times a clear view is obscured. Children are seen as symbolic of fundamental social and psychological issues – the state of the family, the position of parents, male and female roles, deprivation, cruelty and perversion. Children are also social indicators of social policy and thus acquire political significance; this can lead to partial accounts of the way they are treated and of child abuse. When this happens social work can easily become a political instrument rather than a self-evident source of assistance.

This is a momentous time to write a book on children, society and social work. Whatever the outcome of the impending general election, it seems likely that the 1980s are receding in every sense. Although many difficulties lie ahead there are also encouraging opportunities for the State to redefine its relationship with its children. New legislation offers at least a paper balance between protection and promotion; with the addition of a more compassionate political will and extra resources which need not be immense the door is open for a more optimistic, open and collaborative style of social work towards families.

Dingwall et al. (1983) were widely noted for suggesting that social workers in the 1960s and the early 1970s used an unwise *rule of optimism*. This reflected a prevailing social view that children were safe within families. The events of the last twenty years indicate that this lesson has been learnt but that the dominant rule is now one of *pessimism*. For state services the correct position must surely be between these two extremes so we must hope that the next decade achieves the kind of balance which both promotes and protects the welfare of children.

BIBLIOGRAPHY

Ahmad, B. (1989) Child care and ethnic minorities, in B. Kahan (ed.) *Child Care Research, Policy and Practice*. London, Hodder and Stoughton.

Ahmed, S., Cheetham, J. and Small, J. (1986) *Social Work with Black Children and Families* (BAAF). London, Batsford.

Aldgate, J. and Simmonds, J. (1988) *Direct Work with Children*. London, Batsford (BAAF).

Aldgate, J. (1991) Partnership with parents: fantasy or reality?, *Adoption and Fostering*, 15 (2), 5–10.

Allen, C. (1990) Women as perpetrators of sexual abuse: recogniton barriers, in A. Horton, B. Johnson, L. Roundy and D. Williams (eds) *The Incest Perpetrator*. London, Sage.

Allen, N. (1990) *Making Sense of the Children Act 1989*. Harlow, Longman.

Alloway, R. and Bebbington, P. (1987) Buffer theory of social support, *Psychological Medicine*, 17, 91–108.

Amphlett, S. (1988) (Parents Against INjustice – PAIN) *The Parent's Dilemma*. Paper given at Cumberland Lodge 12–14 September. Bishop Stortford, PAIN.

Amphlett, S. (1991) (Parents Against INjustice – PAIN) *Working in Partnership*. Stansted, PAIN.

Aronson, E. (1984) *The Social Animal* (4th edn). New York, W. H. Freeman.

Bainham, A. (1988) *Children, Parents and the State*. London, Sweet and Maxwell.

Bainham, A. (1990) *Children: The New Law, The Children Act 1989*. Bristol, Family Law.

Baker, A. and Duncan, S. (1986) Prevalence of CSA in Great Britain, *Child Abuse and Neglect*, 19, 457–69.

Bamford, T. (1982) *Managing Social Work*. London, Tavistock.

Bannister, A. and Print, B. (1988) *A Model for Assessment Interviews in Suspected Cases of Child Abuse*. Occasional Paper No. 4. London, NSPCC.

Barclay, P. (1982) *Social Workers: their Role and Tasks*. London, Bedford Square Press.

Barr, H. (1990) Measuring up to the EC directive, *Issues in Social Work Education*, 10 (1 and 2), 128–33.

Bebbington, A. and Miles, J. (1989) The background of children who enter local authority care, *British Journal of Social Work*, 19 (5), 349–68.

Bentovim, A. (1991) Significant harm in context, in M. Adcock, R. White and A. Hollows (eds) *Significant Harm*. Croydon, Significant Publications.

Birchall, E. (1989) The frequency of child abuse – what do we really know?, in O. Stevenson (ed.) *Child Abuse*. Hemel Hempstead, Harvester.

Blom-Cooper, L. (1991) Hidden agendas and moral messages: social workers and the press, in B. Franklin and N. Parton (eds) *Social Work, the Media and Public Relations*. London, Routledge.

Bradshaw, J. (1977) The concept of social need, in Fitzgerald et al. (eds) *Welfare in Action*. London, Routledge and Kegan Paul.

Bradshaw, J. (1990) *Child Poverty and Deprivation in the UK*. London, National Children's Bureau.

Brake, M. and Hale, C. (1992) *Public Order and Private Lives*. London, Routledge.

British Association of Social Workers (BASW) (1986) *A Code of Ethics for Social Work*. Birmingham, BASW.

Browne, A. and Finkelhor, D. (1986) Initial and long-term effects: a review of the research, in D. Finkelhor et al. *A Sourcebook on Child Sexual Abuse*. Newbury Park, California, Sage.

Browne, K. (1988) The nature of child abuse and neglect: an overview, in K. Browne, C. Davies and P. Stratton (eds) *Early Prediction and Prevention of Child Abuse*. Chichester, John Wiley.

Brunel Institute of Organization and Social Studies (BIOSS) (1974) *Social Services Departments – Developing Patterns of Work and Organization*. London, Heinemann.

Calam, R. and Franchi, C. (1987) *Child Abuse and its Consequences*. Cambridge, Cambridge University Press.

Campbell, B. (1988) *Unofficial Secrets*. London, Virago Press.

Campbell, B. (1991) Between the lines, *Social Work Today*, 14/11/92, p. 22.

Central Council for Education and Training in Social Work (CCETSW) (1986) *Three Years and Different Routes*, Paper 20.6. London, CCETSW.

CCETSW (1989) *Requirements and Regulations for the Diploma in Social Work*, Paper 30. London, CCETSW.

CCETSW (1991a) *The Teaching of Child Care in the Diploma of Social Work*. London, CCETSW.

CCETSW (1991b) *Right or Privilege: Post-Qualifying Training with Special Reference to Child Care*. London, CCETSW.

Central Statistical Office (1991) *Social Trends 21*. London, HMSO.

Cheetham, J. (1986) Introduction, in S. Ahmed, J. Cheetham and J. Small (eds) *Social Work with Black Children and Families*. London, Batsford (BAAF).

Cohen, B. (1988) *Services and Policies for Child Care and Equal Opportunities in the United Kingdom*. London, Family Policy Studies Centre.

Cooper, D.M. (1982) Chapters 4, 5 and 6, in B. Glastonbury, D.M. Cooper and P. Hawkins *Social Work in Conflict: the Practitioner and the Bureaucrat*. Birmingham, BASW.

Cooper, D.M. and Ball, D. (1987) *Social Work and Child Abuse*. Basingstoke, Macmillan/BASW.

Corby, B. (1987) *Working with Child Abuse*. Milton Keynes, Open University Press.

Corby, B. (1989) Alternative theory bases in child abuse, in W. Stainton Rogers, D. Hevey and E. Ash (eds) *Child Abuse and Neglect*. London, Batsford.

Corby, B. (1991) Sociology, social work and child protection, in M. Davies (ed.) *The Sociology of Social Work*. London, Routledge.

Corrigan, P. and Leonard, P. (1978) *Social Work Practice under Capitalism*. London, Macmillan.

Creighton, S. (1984) *Trends in Child Abuse*. London, NSPCC.

Creighton, S. (1988) The incidence of child abuse and neglect, in K. Browne, C. Davies and P. Stratton (eds) *Early Prediction and Prevention of Child Abuse*. Chichester, John Wiley.

Dale, P. and Davies, M. (1986) *Dangerous Families: Assessment and Treatment of Child Abuse*. London, Tavistock.

Davies, M. (1991) Sociology and social work: a misunderstood relationship, in M. Davies (ed.) *The Sociology of Social Work*. London, Routledge.

De'ath, E. (1989) Families and children, in B. Kahan (ed.) *Child Care Research, Policy and Practice*. London, Hodder and Stoughton.

Department of Employment (1988) *Employment for the 1990s* (White Paper). London, HMSO.

Department of Health (DoH) (1988) *Protecting Children: a Guide for Social Workers Undertaking a Comprehensive Assessment*. London, HMSO.

DoH (1989 and 1990) *Children and Young Persons on Child Protection Registers (Years Ending 31/3/88 and 31/3/89)*. London, Department of Health.

DoH (1991a) *Child Abuse: a Study of Inquiry Reports 1980–1989*. London, HMSO.

DoH (1991b) *Working Together (under the Children Act 1989)*. London, HMSO.

DoH (1991c) *Guidance and Regulations on the Children Act 1989, Vols 1–9*. London, HMSO.

DoH (1991d) *The Pindown Experience and the Protection of Children: The Report of the Staffordshire Child Care Inquiry* (Allan Levy QC and Barbara Kahan). London, HMSO.

DoH (1991e) *Patterns and Outcomes in Child Placement*. London, HMSO.

Department of Health and Social Security (DHSS) (1982) *Child Abuse: a Study of Inquiry Reports 1973–81*. London, HMSO.

DHSS (1985) *Social Work Decisions in Child Care*. London, HMSO.

DHSS (1986) *Child Abuse: Working Together. A Draft Guide to Arrangements for Inter-Agency Co-operation for the Protection of Children*. London, DHSS.

Dingwall, R., Eekelaar, J. and Murray, T. (1983) *The Protection of Children*. Oxford, Blackwell.

Dingwall, R. (1989) Some problems about predicting child abuse, in O. Stevenson (ed.) *Child Abuse*. Hemel Hempstead, Harvester.

Dobash, R. and Dobash, R. (1980) *Violence against Wives: a Case Against the Patriarchy*. London, Open Books.

Dominelli, L. (1988) *Anti-Racist Social Work*. Birmingham, BASW.

Dominelli, L. (1989) Betrayal of trust. A feminine analysis of power relationships in incest abuse and its relevance for social work practice, *British Journal of Social Work*, 19 (4) August, 291–308.

Dominelli, L. and McLeod, E. (1989) *Feminist Social Work*. London and Basingstoke, Macmillan.

Doyle, C. (1990) *Working with Abused Children*. Basingstoke, Macmillan/BASW.

Elliot, M. (1992) Tip of the iceberg, *Social Work Today*, 12/3/92, pp. 12–13.

Faller, K. (1988) *Child Sexual Abuse*. Basingstoke, Macmillan.

Family Rights Group (1991) *The Children Act 1989 – An FRG Briefing Pack*. London, Family Rights Group.

Finer, M. (1974) *Report of the Committee on One-Parent Families* (Cmnd 5629). London, HMSO.

Finkelhor, D. (1984) *Child Sexual Abuse: New Theory and Research*. New York, Free Press.

Finkelhor, D. et al. (1986) *A Sourcebook on Child Sexual Abuse*. London, Sage.

Franklin, B. (ed.) (1986) *The Rights of Children*. Oxford, Blackwell.

Freeman, M. (1991) Reconciling the irreconcilable, *Social Work Today*, 10/10/91, p. 19.

Fromm, E. (1978) *To Have or To Be?* London, Jonathan Cape.

Garbarino, J. (1982) *Children and Families in the Social Environment*. New York, Aldine.

Garbarino, J. and Gillam, G. (1980) *Understanding Abusive Families*. Lexington, Lexington.

Gibbons, J. (1990) *Family Support and Prevention* (National Institute for Social Work). London, HMSO.

Gil, D. (1979) *Child Abuse and Violence*. New York, AMS Press.

Gill, O. and Jackson, B. (1983) *Adoption and Race: Black, Asian and Mixed Race Children in White Families*. London, Batsford.

Glaser, D. and Frosh, S. (1988) *Child Sexual Abuse*. Basingstoke, Macmillan/BASW.

Glasgow, D. (1989) Play-based investigative assessment of children who may have been sexually abused, in C. Wattam, J. Hughes and H. Blagg (eds) *Child Sexual Abuse* (NSPCC). Harlow, Longman.

Glastonbury, B., Cooper, D. M. and Hawkins, P. (1982) *Social Work in Conflict: the Practitioner and the Bureaucrat*. Birmingham, BASW.

Goldberg, E. (1987) *Support for Families: Practice, Policy and Research*. London, Joseph Rowntree Memorial Trust.

Golding, P. (1991) Do-gooders on display: social work, public attitudes and the mass media, in B. Franklin and N. Parton (eds) *Social Work, the Media and Public Relations*. London, Routledge.

Hadley, R. and McGrath, M. (1980) *Going Local*. NCVO Occasional Paper. London, Bedford Square Press.

Hall, S., Critcher, C., Jefferson, T., Clarke, J. and Roberts, B. (1978) *Policing the Crisis: Mugging, the State, and Law and Order*. London, Macmillan.

Hall, S. (1980) *Drifting into a Law and Order Society*. London, Cobden Trust.

Hardiker, P., Exton, K. and Barker, M. (1991) *Policies and Practices in Preventive Child Care*. London, Gower.

Harding, L. Fox. (1991) *Perspectives in Child Care Policy*. London, Longman.

Hoggett, B. (1987) *Parents and Children: The Law of Parental Responsibility*, 3rd edn. London, Sweet and Maxwell.

Hoggett, B. and Pearl, D. (1991) *The Family, Law and Society*. London, Butterworths.

Holman, B. (1988) *Putting Families First: Prevention in Child Care*. Basingstoke, Macmillan.

Home Office (1989) *Report of the Advisory Group on Video-Recorded Evidence*. London, Home Office.

Home Office (1990) *Domestic Violence (Circular 60/90)*. London, Home Office.
Horne, M. (1987) *Values in Social Work* (Community Care Practice Handbook). Aldershot, Wildwood House.
Howe, D. (1986) *Social Workers and their Practice in Welfare Bureaucracies*. Aldershot, Gower.
Howe, D. (1991) Knowledge, power and the shape of social work practice, in M. Davies (ed.) *The Sociology of Social Work*. London, Routledge.
Hudson, P. and Lee, W.R. (eds) (1990) *Women's Work and the Family Economy in Historical Perspective*. Manchester, Manchester University Press.
Illich, I. (1973) *De-Schooling Society*. Harmondsworth, Penguin Books.
Jones, D.P.H. (1991) The effectiveness of intervention, in M. Adcock, R. White and A. Hollows (eds) *Significant Harm*. Croydon, Significant Publications.
Jordan, B. (1974) *Poor Parents: Social Policy and the Cycle of Deprivation*. London, Routledge and Kegan Paul.
Jordan, B. (1987) *Rethinking Welfare*. Oxford, Blackwell.
Jordan, B. (1990) *Social Work in an Unjust Society*. Hemel Hempstead, Harvester Wheatsheaf.
Jordan, B. (1991) Competencies and values, *Social Work Education*, 10 (1), 5–11.
Keane, J. and Owens, J. (1986) *After Full Employment*. London, Hutchinson.
Kelly, L., Regan, L. and Burton, S. (1991) *An Exploratory Study of Sexual Abuse in a Sample of 16–21 Year Olds*. London, Polytechnic of North London.
Kenward, H. and Hevey, D. (1989) The effects of physical abuse and neglect, in W. Stainton Rogers, D. Hevey and E. Ash (eds) *Child Abuse and Neglect*. London, Batsford.
Kotelchuck, M. (1982) Child abuse and neglect: prediction and misclassification, in R. Starr (ed.) *Child Abuse Prediction*. New York, Ballinger.
Lau, A. (1991) Cultural and ethnic perspectives on significant harm: its assessment and treatment, in M. Adcock, R. White and A. Hollows (eds) *Significant Harm*. Croydon, Significant Publications.
Law Commission (1990) *Rape within Marriage*. Working Paper No. 116. London, HMSO.
London Borough of Brent (1985) *A Child in Trust: Report of the Panel of Inquiry Investigating the Circumstances Surrounding the Death of Jasmine Beckford*. London, Borough of Brent.
McBeath, G. and Webb, S. (1990–1) Child protection language and professional ideology in social work, *Social Work and Social Sciences Review*, 2 (2), 122–45.
McEwan, I. (1976) *First Love Last Rites*. London, Picador Pan.
Malucchio, A.N., Fein, E. and Olmstead, K. (1986) *Permanency Planning of Children*. London, Tavistock.
Manning, B. (1988) The London Rape Crisis Centre – a feminist response from the voluntary sector, in *Child Sexual Abuse after Cleveland – Alternative Strategies*. London, Family Rights Group.
Marsh, P. (1989) Substitute care, in B. Kahan (ed.) *Child Care Research, Policy and Practice*. London, Hodder and Stoughton.
Maximé, J. (1986) Some psychological models of black self-concept, in S. Ahmed, J. Cheetham and J. Small (eds) *Social Work with Black Children and Families*. London, Batsford (BAAF).
Milham, S., Bullock, R., Hosie, K. and Haak, M. (1986) *Lost in Care*. Aldershot, Gower.

National Children's Bureau/Barnardos (1991) *Children as Witnesses*. Highlight No. 104. London, National Children's Bureau.

Norrie, A. and Adelman, S. (1989) 'Consensual authoritarianism' and criminal justice, in A. Gamble and C. Wells (eds) *Thatcher's Law*. Oxford, Blackwell.

O'Hagan, K. (1989) *Working with Child Sexual Abuse*. Milton Keynes, Open University Press.

O'Hagan, K. (1992) *Emotional and Psychological Abuse of Children*. Buckingham, Open University Press.

Okri, B. (1991) *The Famished Road*. London, Jonathan Cape.

Oppenheim, C. (1990) *Poverty: the Facts*. London, Child Poverty Action Group.

Packman, J. (1981) *The Child's Generation* (2nd edn). Oxford, Blackwell.

Packman, J., Randall, J. and Jacques, N. (1986) *Who Needs Care? Social Work Decisions about Children*. Oxford, Blackwell.

Pahl, J. (ed.) (1985) *Private Violence and Public Policy: the Needs of Battered Women and the Response of the Public Service*. London, Routledge and Kegan Paul.

Parents Against INjustice (PAIN) (1990) *Report and Recommendations on Voluntary and Compulsory Ousting*. Bishop Stortford, PAIN.

Parents Against INjustice (PAIN) (1991) *Press Conference Release Report* (Rochdale, 1990; Orkney, 1991). Bishop Stortford, PAIN.

Parker, R. (1990) *Safeguarding Standards*. London, National Institute for Social Work.

Parton, C. and Parton, N. (1989) Child protection: the law and dangerousness, in O. Stevenson (ed.) *Child Abuse*. Hemel Hempstead, Harvester.

Parton, N. (1985) *The Politics of Child Abuse*. Basingstoke, Macmillan.

Parton, N. (1991) *Governing the Family*. Basingstoke, Macmillan.

Pearson, G. (1975) *The Deviant Imagination: Psychiatry, Social Work and Social Change*. London, Macmillan.

Pfohl, S. (1977) The discovery of child abuse, *Social Problems*, 24, 310–23.

Pinker, R. (1986) Time to stop CCETSW in its tracks, *Community Care*, 9/8/86, pp. 21–22.

Pizzey, E. (1974) *Scream Quietly or the Neighbours will Hear*. Harmondsworth, Penguin.

Pringle, K. (1990) *Managing to Survive*. Newcastle-upon-Tyne, Barnardos.

Postman, N. (1987) *Amusing Ourselves to Death*. London, Methuen.

Roche, J. (1989) Children's rights and the welfare of the child, in W. Stainton Rogers, D. Hevey and E. Ash (eds.) *Child Abuse and Neglect*. London, Batsford.

Rowe, J. and Lambert, L. (1973) *Children who Wait*. London, Association of British Adoption Agencies.

Rowe, J., Cain, H., Hundleby, M. and Keane, A. (1984) *Long-Term Foster Care*. London, Batsford.

Sale, A. and Davies, M. (eds) (1990) *Child Protection Policies and Practice in Europe*. London, NSPCC.

Sapey, B. (1992) Community care – empowerment or social death, *Grapevine*. Devon BASW magazine, No. 29, February.

Schecter, M. and Roberge, L. (1976) Sexual exploitation, in R. Helfer and C. Kempe (eds) *Child Abuse and Neglect: The Family and the Community*. Cambridge, Mass., Ballinger.

Search, G. (1988) *The Last Taboo*. London, Penguin.

Secretary of State for Social Services (1988) *Report of the Inquiry into Child Abuse in Cleveland* (Cmnd 412). London, HMSO.

Seebohm, Lord (1968) *Report of the Committee on Local Authority and Allied Personal Social Services*. London, HMSO.

Sheppard, M. (1982) *Perceptions of Child Abuse: a Critique of Individualism* (Social Work Monograph). Norwich, University of East Anglia.

Sibeon, R. (1991) The construction of a contemporary sociology of social work, in M. Davies (ed.) *The Sociology of Social Work*. London, Routledge.

Simpkin, M. (1979) *Trapped within Welfare*. London, Macmillan.

Sluckin, A. and Dolan, R. (1989) Tackling child abuse in the EC, *Social Work Today*, 31/8/89, pp. 14–15.

Smith, D. (1991) The ties that bind, *Social Work Today*, 28/11/91, pp. 20–21.

Social Services Inspectorate (1990) *Inspection of Child Protection Services in Rochdale*. London, Department of Health, HMSO.

Starr, R. (ed.) (1982) *Child Abuse Prediction: Policy Implications*. Cambridge, Ballinger.

Stein, T. J., and Rzepnicki, T. (1983) *Decision Making at Child Welfare Intake*. New York, Child Welfare League of America.

Stevenson, O. (1989) Multidisciplinary work in child protection, in O. Stevenson (ed.) *Child Abuse*. Hemel Hempstead, Harvester.

Taylor, S. (1989) How prevalent is it?, in W. Stainton Rogers, D. Hevey, and E. Ash (eds) *Child Abuse and Neglect*. London, Batsford.

Thorman, G. (1982) *Helping Troubled Families*. New York, Aldine.

Underwager, R. (1987) *Statement to the Cleveland Inquiry*. Bishops Stortford, Parents Against INjustice.

Van Montfoort, A. (1990) *Reporting Child Abuse in the Netherlands*. Paper to the 8th International Congress on Child Abuse and Neglect. Hamburg, West Germany, 2–6 September.

Van der Eyken, W. (1982) *Home-Start – A Four Year Evaluation*. Leicester, Home-Start Consultancy.

Wakefield, H. and Underwager, R. (1988) *Accusations of Child Sexual Abuse*. Springfield, Illinois, C. C. Thomas.

Walton, M. (1989) What use are statistics? – policy and practice in child abuse, in C. Wattam, J. Hughes and H. Blagg (eds) *Child Sexual Abuse* (NSPCC). Harlow, Longman.

Webb, D. (1990–1) Puritans and paradigms: a speculation on the form of new moralities in social work, *Social Work and Social Sciences Review*, 2 (2), 146–59.

Wells, J. (1989) Powerplays – considerations in communicating with children, in C. Wattam, J. Hughes and H. Blagg (eds) *Child Sexual Abuse* (NSPCC). Harlow, Longman.

White, R. (1990) Family Practice, *New Law Journal*, 25/5/90, pp. 748–9.

Whittaker, J. and Garbarino, J. (1983) *Social Support Networks: Informal Helping in the Human Services*. New York: Aldine.

Williams, F. (1989) *Social Policy – A Critical Introduction*. Cambridge, Polity Press.

Wolfers, O. (1992) Same abuse, different parent, *Social Work Today*, 12/3/92, pp. 13–14.

Wyre, R. (1989) Gracewell Clinic, in W. Stainton Rogers, D. Hevey and E. Ash (eds) *Child Abuse and Neglect*. London, Batsford.

INDEX